Church of Birds

An Eco-History of Myth and Religion

Church of Birds

An Eco-History of Myth and Religion

Ben H Gagnon

**MOON
BOOKS**

Winchester, UK
Washington, USA

JOHN HUNT PUBLISHING

First published by Moon Books, 2023
Moon Books is an imprint of John Hunt Publishing Ltd., No. 3 East Street, Alresford
Hampshire SO24 9EE, UK
office@jhpbooks.net
www.johnhuntpublishing.com
www.moon-books.net

For distributor details and how to order please visit the 'Ordering' section on our website.

ISBN: 978 1 80341 122 4
978 1 80341 123 1 (ebook)
Library of Congress Control Number: 2022932510

Design: Matthew Greenfield

UK: Printed and bound by CPI Group (UK) Ltd, Croydon, CR0 4YY
Printed in North America by CPI GPS partners

We operate a distinctive and ethical publishing philosophy in
all areas of our business, from our global network of authors to
production and worldwide distribution.

Contents

Previous Titles

People of the Flow: A Personal Journey
into Ireland's Ancient Past
October 2019, Beacon Publishing Group, Charleston SC.
ISBN: 978-1-949472-64-6.

Introduction

There are dozens of science-based books about the behavior and intelligence of birds, and every year or two a book is published on avian mythology and symbolism. *Church of Birds* combines modern science and ancient myth to tell a long-forgotten story about the profound bond between humans and birds, a story much older than previously imagined.

Bird migration mapping, the human fossil record, and recent scientific studies show that our most distant ancestors consistently chose to live in prime bird habitat, a wise choice for an opportunistic species that was itself migratory. The earliest farmers settled in the prime bird habitat of serpentine river systems fed by the headwaters of volcanic mountain ranges. Before the advent of Judaism and Christianity, it was a nearly universal condition to perceive migratory birds as divine agents and messengers of the sun, delivering seeds every spring and carrying souls to heaven in autumn.

Describing highlights from the chapters ahead is ideally meant to get the juices flowing but it's also a courtesy, so readers can decide if they're interested in proceeding. Highlights only become a problem when they're too bizarre for the average reader. For example, is it believable that across the ancient world it was common for women to reach full term and give birth during the weeklong winter solstice ceremonies, with reason to believe their child would grow up to be a hero or a king? Why haven't I heard of that before?

Across the ancient world, spring equinox festivals actively promoted widespread intercourse, an activity fully endorsed by the sacred calendar, celebrated with lascivious poetry, and in one case featuring a giant wooden phallus carted through the fields. It suddenly becomes more believable that nine months later, the celebration of the sun's rebirth during the weeklong winter solstice festivities was also the time on the sacred calendar for women to give birth.

Natural selection may have produced this phenomenon, favoring hunter-gatherers who gave birth in mid-winter when the group was in a settled environment rather than warmer seasons when they were on the move. Legends of heroes and gods being born on the winter solstice may have served as motivation during the spring sex-festivals: *Let's lie in the verdant fields my love and make a demi-god!* (There are other aspects to this scenario that are withheld for now because it would spoil the fun.)

Meanwhile, it's fair to say the coming chapters are filled with recent scientific discoveries that confirm the accuracy of beliefs expressed in the ancient myths of cultures around the world. Most myths were symbolic expressions of what people believed to be true about the natural world around them, the universe of the night sky, how it all began, how it worked, and what happened after mortal death. Creation myths celebrated birds teaching humans how to speak and recounted the original delivery of seeds to the land by migratory birds appearing from beyond the horizon. Both beliefs were found to be accurate, according to scientific and scholarly studies published in the last decade. Linguistic and genetic studies at separate universities have linked birdsong to the origins and development of human language. Another study found that migratory birds carry enough viable seeds over long distances to diversify the flora on their seasonal grounds. The ancient belief in seed-bearing birds was likely among the reasons why the fossil record reflects people following their migration routes. Wherever the birds went every winter would be another bountiful garden. It appears our distant ancestors wisely perceived birds as indicators of biodiversity and told mythic tales celebrating the bountiful ecosystems in which they both lived.

Across cultures, perhaps the most common mythic role played by birds was intermediary between the material world on earth and the spirit world of the heavens. Certain sacred bird species were believed to play crucial roles in the process of reincarnation and preserving the immortal soul. The sacred theater once performed during periods of bird migration released the souls of the dead to join the birds on their journey beyond the horizon. These dramatic moments are part of a long-lost eco-history recounted in the coming chapters that follows a wide trail of evidence, while leaving plenty of room for the reader's imagination to wander.

Chapter 1

The Language of Birdsong

In June 2013, the Massachusetts Institute of Technology (MIT) made international headlines with a linguistic study concluding that human language developed by imitating the melodies of birdsong. Copying the lyrical, melodic phrases of birdsong allowed for a wider range of human expression, leading to more sophisticated social organization. In 2014, a genetic study at Duke University confirmed that humans and birds share an identical set of about 50 genes that are activated when birds learn to sing and humans learn to talk. In *The Descent of Man* (1871), Charles Darwin wrote, "The sounds uttered by birds offer in several respects the nearest analogy to language ... I cannot doubt that language owes its origins to the imitation and modification of various natural sounds..."

MIT, Duke, and Darwin were late to the party. Birdsong was linked with the origin of human language in creation stories from Africa to Asia and the Americas. In the Hopi story of creation, the mockingbird led Native Americans out from the Underworld and gave each tribe a language. The Osage of Kansas say their ancestral souls were once without bodies until a redbird volunteered that its own body could be used to make human children by transforming its wings into arms and its beak into a nose. The redbird concluded with the gift of language. "The speech of children will I bestow on your children." The Bambara of southern Mali, Guinea, and Senegal tell of the crested crane uttering two words at the birth of language, "I speak." In ancient Egypt, the voice of the ibis-headed god Thoth caused the cosmic egg to hatch. The vocalizations of birds coincide with the emergence of humans in creation myths from Africa to Asia and North America:

- The Wapangwa of Tanzania say the wind and air gave birth to singing birds that descended to earth and turned into people and animals.
- On the island of Borneo, the Iban say two birds shaped earth into people and brought them to life with bird calls.
- In Japanese myth, the roosters of the Eternal Land crowed when the Sun Goddess and Storm God created people.
- The Seri tribe of the Gulf of California believe the Ancient of Pelicans created the world with supernatural wisdom and melodious song.

If early humans developed language by imitating birdsong, it's nothing short of incredible that this fact ended up symbolically expressed in creation myths several hundred thousand years after the fact, from Africa to Kansas. Linking birdsong with human language may have been similar to the deep intuition that inspired the Roman poet and philosopher Lucretius to accurately describe the nature of atoms more than 2,000 years ago. Creation myths could have told a story of humans teaching birds how to sing, but instead assumed (correctly) that birds and bird language preceded humans on the evolutionary tree. (As it turns out, birds evolved from dinosaurs about 150 million years ago.)

Did each culture independently link birdsong to language or was the concept diffused across cultures and time? Likely some of both. More importantly, those who authored and passed on these creation myths perceived a deep and fundamental connection between humans and birds, accompanied by what must have been a profound sense of awe and respect for certain bird species that were considered sacred. The mysterious wisdom of bird language was celebrated around the world and down through the millennia in creation myths, folktales, and legends.

In the mystical traditions of both the Hebrew Kabbalah and the Sufi branch of Islam, the secret language of birds holds the key to knowledge and wisdom. Bird language was known by King Solomon, the Greek god Heracles, the prophetess Cassandra, the Oracle at Dodona, and the Greek philosopher Democritus. The Norse god Odin and the sun god Apollo had a pair of ravens who kept them informed of human events. In Egyptian Arabic, hieroglyphs are known as "the alphabet of the birds." The ancient Greeks based four letters (lambda, delta, upsilon, and psi) on the flight formations of cranes.

The prestige and authority of healers and shamanic figures depended on their knowledge of bird language. A Greek myth tells of the esteemed physician Melampus, who was able to treat his patients only after listening to a pair of vultures sitting nearby, chatting about the best cure. The dialogue between the vultures was quite specific, and because Melampus knew the language of birds, he simply followed their advice. When Apollo sent a plague to the Greeks in the *Iliad*, they turned to "the best expert on birds, who knew things present, future, and past." After listening to birds, the expert called for a sacrifice to Apollo and the plague stopped. When Jason and the Argonauts were stranded on a windless day, the crew took the advice of a twittering kingfisher and made an offering to the goddess Rhea. The winds picked up.

In folk tales from Wales to Russia, heroes who performed a good deed for a bird were rewarded with the knowledge of bird language. A Scottish legend tells of a chief who set out to disprove a local superstition that a boy who drinks from a raven's skull will learn bird language. But after drinking from a raven's skull the boy began conversing with birds. As a young man, he convinced a group of sparrows to stop bothering the king of France, who rewarded him with a ship and crew. It was said he grew wealthy and built a castle in the western highlands.

A bizarre story of how a dove passed its knowledge to a pope in the late 6th century was recorded in *The Catholic Encyclopedia* by Pope Gregory I's secretary, who wrote that he observed the pope with a living dove's beak between his lips. When the dove

6

removed its beak, the pope began dictating to the secretary, who was supposed to be out of sight behind a curtain.

The widespread belief that birds had knowledge of the future was a primary reason why it was so important to understand their language. Cross-cultural legends describe a bird "announcing" a person's imminent death by appearing on a doorstep or calling outside a window. This foundation of bird mythology may have developed from the observation of entire flocks scattering on a sunny day for no apparent reason, until four or five hours later when the reason became clear: A Category 5 hurricane knocked over mature trees, triggered landslides, and started a raging flood. Quite a memorable event. How did the birds know it was coming? In at least two instances in recent years, ornithologists tracking bird migration have recorded entire flocks stopping suddenly and returning from where they originated to avoid catastrophic storms hundreds of miles ahead. It turns out birds perceive dramatic changes in barometric pressure and can hear the low frequency rumble of thunder hundreds of miles away. Without the mantle of scientific knowledge, it's no great surprise our distant ancestors concluded birds could predict the future. The Romans once wrote letters on seed kernels, tossed them on the ground, and divined the future based on the order that birds picked them up.

The Very Vocal Whooper Swan

In ancient Ireland, the god of eloquence was Ogma, once depicted in a painting with a slender golden chain connecting his tongue to the ears of two or three men following him. Describing the scene, the 1st century Syrian writer Lucian commented that "… they look like men who would be grieved should they be set free." It seems the gold chain that tied Ogma's tongue to his followers' ears was a symbol of eloquence. In Irish myth, the same slender gold chain symbolically connected the necks of whooper swans together as they sang.

Ogma was a member of the *Tuatha Dé* Danann (tribe of Danu), known in Irish legend as the first people to bring poetry and music to Ireland. A fair guess is the Danann arrived about 3,500 years ago in the Boyne Valley (County Meath), where they found three abandoned megalithic mounds and a flock of seasonal whooper swans. They named one of the mounds Brú na Bóinne, home of the chief Dagda. Perhaps the most famous Danann legend comes from an 8th century text describing Ogma's brother Angus falling in love with a woman who had a habit of shapeshifting into a swan. Pursuing his true love, Angus found her as a swan, bound together with other swans by thin golden chains around their throats, from which their music came. Angus then turned himself into a swan to join his love, and the pair flew off singing with joy, connected with a slender golden chain. When they arrived back in the Boyne Valley, the pair sang so beautifully that listeners fell into a deep, soothing sleep.

In *The Whooper Swan* (2003), ornithologist Mark Brazil found the whooper to be the most vocal and intelligent of all swan species, raising young at a remarkable success rate of 85 percent. When two whoopers meet after a time apart, their greeting begins with a long duet that morphs into both singing the same song in perfect synchrony. When the calling ends, the pair flap their wings and rush together. During the day, a flock will "talk" in short, high-pitched tones while at night the conversation is soft, mostly twittering and trilling.

Myths about the whooper are found in cultures across its habitat, from western Europe to the Mediterranean and Scandinavia, eastern Europe, Central Asia, Siberia, China, and Japan. The Greek historian Diodorus Siculus wrote that whoopers and people once sang together harmoniously on a mythical island known as Hyperborea in the "far north." Siculus described swans circling a temple on the spring equinox "as though they were making a ceremonial purification of the building with their wings..." When the human chorus sang and the musicians played, "...the swans made their concordant music, not losing time or tune, as though they had got the keynote from the choir conductor, and were joining their natural music with that of the artists of the sacred minstrelsy; and then, when the hymn ends, away they fly..." In Greek paintings and mosaics, swans were shown singing along while men played the lyre. A medieval French bestiary praised the ability of swans to harmonize with the harp.

Ancient Flutes and Birdsong

Among the world's oldest musical instruments, the flute has long been used to imitate songbirds. A five-hole flute made 42,000 years ago from the wing bone of a griffon vulture was found in 2008 inside Hohle Fels Cave in southern Germany. The instrument may well have been played in the echoing cave where it was found, and for a sacred purpose. In a cave in southern France, archaeologists discovered flute fragments made from the wing bones of swans between 26,000 and 32,000 years ago near Isturlitz, by the coast.

In Papua New Guinea, the Gimi language uses the same word for bird and flute (*nimi*). An ancient tradition across New Guinea involves men playing flutes so that women and children can hear the music but not see the players. The intended effect is for listeners to believe they're hearing the songs of mysterious, supernatural birds.

In Chinese legend, the Yellow Emperor sends his aide Linglun on a journey to find musical instruments for sacred ceremonies. Asleep in the forest, Linglun is awakened by the song of two phoenixes perched in a tree. Seeking to imitate the beautiful music, Linglun fashioned a piece of bamboo into a musical pipe and produced the first 12-note musical scale. A 9,000-year-old flute found in Henan Province, the cradle of Chinese civilization, was played again at a ceremony in 1999, making it the oldest playable flute in the world.

A legend of the *Brulé* Sioux tribe in Wyoming describes a young man who dreamt of a singing woodpecker and awoke the next morning to see a woodpecker singing the song in his dream. The bird flew off a little way and the young man followed until they arrived in a clearing where the hollow trunk of a dead tree lay on the ground. The woodpecker had made regular holes up and down the length of the hollow log, and as the wind rose and blew through the hollow log, beautiful melodies emerged. The young man learned to make and play the flute and won over his sweetheart with his music. Soon all the men of the *Brulé* Sioux were making flutes. In the Great Lakes region, it was said that Ojibwe flute music was inspired by the call of the loon. The Shastans of central California credit the falcon with inventing the flute.

The naturalist Pliny wrote of a funeral procession in Rome to honor a beloved raven that was hatched from a nest atop the temple of Castor and Pollux, noting the procession was longer than many held for esteemed senators. At the front of the long trail of mourners was a flute player, followed by two Ethiopians carrying the raven's funeral pyre.

Classical scholars gave birds credit for inspiring the first musicians. The Greek Athenaeus wrote, "... the invention of music was conceived by the ancients from the sounds of birds singing in the wild." In his classic *On the Nature of Things*, the Roman philosopher Lucretius wrote, "Thus birds instructed man, and taught them songs before their art began." Birdsong was also associated with Beethoven, Mozart, and other classical composers. Beethoven was quoted telling a friend that he wrote the *Scene at the Brook* on one of his daily walks, with "the yellowhammers above, the quails, nightingales, and cuckoos all around, compos(ing) with me." In one of Mozart's journals, he wrote of teaching his pet starling to sing the opening theme of a piano concerto. Mozart was so fond of the bird that he held a funeral when it died and composed *A Sextet for Strings and Two*

Horns that resembled the starling's song.

Birds in Popular Music

From seagulls to crows and the disco duck, birds have been used for band names and song titles for generations in modern western culture, from *The Byrds* to *The Yardbirds, Atomic Rooster, The Partridge Family, Paul McCartney & Wings, The Eagles, A Flock of Seagulls, The Black Crowes,* and *Counting Crows.* Some of the most memorable rock 'n roll songs invoke the mythic avian quality of transporting the soul.

- *Lynryd Skynyrd's* "Free Bird" peaked at #19 on the Top 40 in January 1975. It's one of *Rolling Stone's* 500 Greatest Songs of All Time.
- "Fly Like an Eagle" by *The Steve Miller Band* rose to #2 on the Billboard Hot 100 in 1976/'77 and returned in 1997 when Seal's version rose to #10. *Birds & Blooms* magazine crowned it "the best-ever song about birds."
- In 1984, "When Doves Cry" hit #1 on the Billboard Hot 100 and stayed there for five weeks. It's one of *Rolling Stone's* 500 Greatest Songs of All Time. Prince kept two mourning doves named Majesty and Divinity. In folk tales, the mourning dove symbolized the soul of a deceased relative or friend come to comfort the living.
- The mourning dove, a migratory bird that frequents New York State, was the bird perched on the neck of a guitar on the poster advertising the Woodstock concert in August 1969.

The Oldest Language?

Most scholars have long assumed that Neanderthals used some form of language, but the proof was elusive until the recent publication of three studies: 1) Analysis of the hypoglossal canal and hyoid bone in the lower part of a Neanderthal skull found in Kebara Cave in Israel suggested the vocal apparatus was similar to modern humans, 2) Genetic studies in the early 2000s found that Neanderthals had the FOXP2 gene, believed to be responsible for speech and language, and 3) A 2021 analysis of audio-related bones in the inner ear of Neanderthals published in *Nature Ecology & Evolution* claims "that Neanderthals evolved the auditory capacities to support a vocal communication system as efficient as modern human speech." For all we know today, Neanderthals also imitated birds.

The Max Planck Institute for Psycholinguistics at Nijmegen recently concluded that spoken language was likely practiced at least 600,000 years ago by *Homo heidelbergensis* and may have emerged more than a million years ago. The institute cited the continual widening of the hominin nerve canal controlling the tongue and a steady increase in the size of the cerebral cortex, which governs speech and social cues. Leaving open the possibility of language developing more than a million years ago means the institute suspects *Homo erectus* also spoke a language. Archaeologists have found that *Homo erectus* brains kept getting bigger over time. When they died out as recently as 50,000 years ago, their brain size exceeded 1000 cm3, the same as the smallest humans. Whether *Homo erectus* spoke a language may be less a question of scientific proof than a matter of common sense. Would it be possible for a human-like species to trek thousands of miles over unknown territory and spread sustainable populations across Africa, the Mediterranean region, the Near East, India, Southeast Asia, and northeast China, all without engaging in oral communication? Or singing songs to pass the time?

Chapter 2

Planting the Gardens of Eden

Charles Darwin had a hunch that migratory birds were responsible for delivering the seeds of vegetation around the world, but his efforts to design a reliable test proved fruitless. In September 2012, a team of scientists picked up where the father of evolution left off.

Migratory birds flying southwest from Europe are exhausted by the time they arrive in the Canary Islands off West Africa, where they become the hapless prey of the Eleanora falcon, which makes a pile of the dead near its nest for later consumption. It was a perfect chance to put Darwin's theory to the test, to determine whether migratory birds carry seeds in their guts. When the Eleanora falcons took off for their morning hunt, a team of scientists went straight for the piles of dead migratory birds and surgically removed their digestive tracts, kindly leaving the remainder of the corpses for the falcons. Back in the lab, the evidence showed the dead birds had enough viable seeds in their bellies to substantially increase the diversity of flora on their seasonal grounds. The findings were confirmed when the experiment was repeated in 2013, and three years later the study made headlines when it was published in *The Royal Society of Biology* in London. The Canary Islands team of scientists deserved to raise their glasses in a toast. They had identified seed-bearing migratory birds as a substantial "vector of dispersal" in the development of biodiverse landscapes. But they had no way of knowing their discovery would shed light on a missing chapter of human eco-history.

The Science of Ancient Myth

Not only was it common knowledge among ancient cultures that migratory birds delivered seeds to the landscape each spring, it was celebrated as a sacred act of benevolence that first occurred at the time of Creation. Birds were said to deliver the seeds of everything from rice to squash, peanuts, fruit, beans, corn, tobacco, and trees.

- The Kaonde of Zambia say honey birds brought seeds to the first humans.
- In Persian myth the Simurgh bird shook the seeds of all plants from the tree of life.
- In northeast China, magpies dropped the first fruits on the earth.
- In eastern China, a Jiangnan myth says sparrows stole rice from heaven for humans.
- In Greek myth, a dove flew an olive leaf to the Acropolis, where it grew into a tree.
- In the Great Lakes area, the Algonquin told of crows bringing the first seeds to the land.
- In the southeastern U.S., Choctaw legend says birds brought maize to the tribe.
- The Navajo described turkeys rescuing the seeds of all plants from a flood.
- The Hidatsa of North Dakota believed geese brought corn in the spring while ducks delivered beans and swans carried squash seeds.
- The White Mountain Apache say a turkey gave seeds to hungry young children, told them where to plant them.
- In the Caribbean, the Arawak say hummingbirds brought tobacco seeds from the heavens.

Numerous cultures went a step further and gave credit to various birds for creating the landscape itself.

- The Edo of Benin say a bird spread earth over the primordial waters.

- The Yoruba of West Africa say the son of the sky god descended with a chicken and sand to create soil.
- In northern Japan, the Ainu tell of a water wagtail who made land by packing bits of soggy earth together, stomping on them with its feet, and beating them with its tail.
- In eastern Siberia, the Koryak describe a raven god dropping a feather that created the Kamchatka Peninsula.
- In northern California the Maidu say that Earth-Maker and Old Man Coyote found the nest of a meadowlark and stretched it out to form the Earth.
- The Cherokee and Seneca tribes of the Great Lakes region tell of a buzzard stirring up the flat earth and making mountains and valleys by beating its wings.

Birds were perceived as the divine heralds of spring, delivering exotic seeds and producing bountiful landscapes year after year, a perception now shown to be scientifically accurate. The divine status of migratory birds may have been cemented by the notion that birds delivered the seeds of medicinal plants. Before Buddhism reached Tibet, the semi-legendary King Gesar flew to the heavens on the back of a bird to obtain healing herbs. In Nigeria, Yoruban herbalists carry a staff with a bird on top. Hindu cosmology describes an eagle-falcon bringing the healing drink known as soma to the injured. Across the globe, there's a correlation between some of the largest seasonal grounds of migratory birds and the gathering and/or domestication of medicinal plants. Birds from across the United States winter on the Yucatan Peninsula, a hotspot of biodiversity where more than 600 plants are registered as medicinal. Considered the cradle of Chinese civilization, Henan Province is the winter ground for millions of birds and also home to the country's largest medicinal plant factory. Southern Peru is a massive winter ground for migratory birds where dozens of medical and psychoactive plants have been used for untold millennia.

Trekking with Birds: A Case of Natural Selection

Year after year, watching millions of birds fly away in late fall, following the sun and carrying seeds to some unknown destination beyond the horizon, it was only a matter of time before our distant ancestors decided to follow them.

Perhaps a natural catastrophe or dramatic climate change led to a simple deduction: *If migratory birds deliver the seeds of the bountiful land we share six months a year, wherever they fly every winter should also be full of life.* There are several reasons why following migratory bird routes would have substantially improved the chances of a group of people surviving an extended trek. Most importantly bird migration routes don't stray far from fresh water and fertile ecosystems with plentiful resources. For their own benefit, some bird species actually guide people to food. Crows and ravens lead hunters to wounded prey, hoping to feast on scraps. In Africa, the honeyguide leads bushmen to beehives to scare away the bees and retrieve the honey while the birds eat the beeswax. *Homo erectus* may have followed the honeyguide bird, as fossil remains dating back 1.75 million years in East Africa revealed a bone disease caused by eating too much honey. Of course, circling vultures often indicate a nearby carcass. Another important advantage of being among a high population of birds are their alarm calls, which warn of predators nearby. It's a simple matter to learn bird alarm calls, which are taught in wilderness trekking courses. Also, the scattering behavior of birds is an indicator that a hurricane and/or tornados are on the way, even if there are no visible signs. Finally, birds and their eggs make for nutritious meals.

The choice to follow birds and live among large bird populations was an open and shut case of natural selection. In the company of birds the human trekker was more likely to find fresh water and food while enjoying a 24/7 security system that warned of predators and cataclysmic storms. Those who didn't follow busy bird routes were more likely to die of thirst, hunger, predators, or flooding.

The maker of the 42,000-year-old flute in Hohle Fels Cave in southwestern Germany was likely part of a wave of early humans arriving in Europe from Africa at the time. Was it coincidence that the flute was made from the wing bone of a vulture and discovered where two bird migration routes converge? Or had the flutemaker and his or her companions been following birds all along?

Mythic Migrations

A rich vein of myth and legend tells of people following the guidance of birds on long-range treks. In Virgil's *Aeneid,* Venus gave her son Aeneas two doves in his search for a magic golden bough he planned to give as a gift to the goddess Persephone. The doves led him through a deep forest to a tree with a golden bough near a volcanic crater at the entrance to the underworld. When Jason and the Argonauts approached the Clashing Rocks, they released a dove to see if it could get through. The dove flew through the perilous boulders with only a slightly clipped tail, and Jason's ship followed, losing only the tip of its prop.

Some stories about following birds were recorded as true events. After the Greek island of Santorini was destroyed by a volcanic eruption about 3,600 years ago, it was said that ravens guided the people of Thera across the Aegean Sea to their new home in modern-day Libya. About 2,300 years ago, a Celtic tribe followed the flight of migrating birds across Illyria (the Western Balkans), according to the Roman Emperor Justinian. In Plutarch's *Life of Alexander,* a flock of ravens came to the rescue of Alexander's army and put them back on course. "When the guides became confused over the landmarks and the travelers got separated, lost their way and started wandering about, ravens appeared and took over the role of guiding them on their journeys," Plutarch wrote. "They flew swiftly in front for them to follow, but then waited for them if they slowed down and lagged behind. What was most remarkable of all, we're told, was that they called out to those who strayed away at night and by their croaking set them back on the right track." Another legend tells of ravens guiding Alexander through the deserts of Libya to an oasis where he consulted the Oracle of Amun.

Before the Viking mariner Flóki set off on his 9th century journey over unknown seas to the west, he performed a ritual intended to join his soul with three ravens. Danish scholar Wilhelm Gronbech wrote that Flóki was made into a "raven-man (who) flew with unerring instinct over the sea." After passing the last known island west of Norway, Flóki released a raven that flew back to Norway. A few days later a second was released but returned to the ship. Finally, Flóki released the last raven, which led him to Iceland. On the first voyage of Hernando Cortez to America the crew was low on both food and water on Good Friday when a dove came flying along and perched on the mast. The crew cheered "and all gave heartie thanks to God, directing their course the way the Dove flew."

The Volcano Road

Where birds went, people followed. Today, ever-more sophisticated bird migration maps can be helpful tools in tracing the steps of our distant ancestors.

Ornithologists believe the eight global bird migration flyways are likely to be virtually the same today as they were 2.7 million years ago when the continents took their current form, largely because migratory birds take the most energy-efficient routes, riding thermal uplifts along coastlines and over mountain ranges. Birds avoid large bodies of water because they act as "heat sinks" that make it harder to fly. When crossing the Mediterranean migratory birds make regular stopovers on islands such as Sicily and Malta. The only changes in bird routes occur when they extend farther north during global warming and farther south when the planet cools. Each global flyway carries a different mix of about 300 migratory bird species, with the exception of the East Asia/Australasia Flyway, which carries nearly 500 species. Much like a highway system, each flyway is interconnected with sub-routes. Smaller birds travel thousands of miles while some raptors migrate only a few hundred miles.

Where two bird flyways overlap, the variety of migratory species doubles along with the population. The convergence of three flyways is a rare occurrence found in only six parts of the globe, south of the Arctic Circle: 1) the Eurasian Steppe, including the Caucasus Mountains, 2) a swath of territory running north-south from Chad to South Africa, 3) the Hudson Bay region, 4) parts of Central America, including the Yucatan Peninsula, Honduras, Nicaragua, and Panama, 5) the tip of South America, and 6) most of Alaska. In these regions the seasonal migratory bird population is massive and extremely diverse, with almost 1,000 species represented. An even greater level of avian diversity is found where four flyways converge over north-central Russia while even further north near the coast of the Arctic Ocean a fifth flyway tips the scales.

Prime bird habitat is also found throughout the world on small to modest-sized islands that are often predator-free, featuring meandering coastlines and coves, making them perfect stopover sites or seasonal grounds. There are 6,000 islands in the oceans surrounding the British Isles and Ireland and the skies above are like Grand Central Station for migratory birds, with routes coming and going in all four cardinal directions twice a year. A similar phenomenon occurs over Greece (6,000 islands), Southeast Asia (25,000 islands), and Japan (7,000 islands). The visual impact of birds in island regions is magnified by the presence of large waterfowl, from swans to flamingos.

A close study of bird flyways and sub-routes shows they often cross through volcanic areas, sometimes following them for extended distances, including the entire length of the Pacific Ring of Fire. A 2007 study at the University of Oldenburg, Germany, found that birds perceive magnetism in their visual cortex. Due to the extreme heating and subsequent cooling of iron-rich magma, volcanic areas are permanently magnetic. If birds can "see" magnetism in their visual cortex, they would recognize it equally well on a pitch-black night or in a thunderstorm, making volcanos the perfect immovable signposts for long-distance migrations. For now, the theory that volcanic regions are a magnetic guide for birds is unproven. The level of magnetism birds can perceive and from what distance, has yet to be identified and calibrated.

Even if birds don't use volcanic magnetism as a navigational aid, there are several other good reasons why multiple flyways and seasonal grounds often coincide with volcanic regions: 1) Thermal uplift from geothermal heat makes flying easier, 2) Volcanic eruptions perpetually recharge the soil and produce water-retaining ash, supporting a consistent supply of vegetative food sources, and 3) Volcanic islands are ideal, often predator-free stopover sites to eat and rest when flying over water.

Over vast expanses of time, the fertile volcanic soil beneath multiple global flyways was further enriched each year by bird droppings containing nitrates and phosphates. By introducing exotic seeds into the volcanic mix, migratory birds were the final piece of a perfect ecological storm that transformed their seasonal grounds into hotspots of biodiversity. A wider variety of vegetation meant more insects and frogs, snakes, rodents, and finally mammals. A comprehensive review of landscapes where hominin (human-like species) fossils have been found shows a clear preference for areas where multiple bird migration flyways converge over sharply bending serpentine rivers with islands, marshes, and one or more tributaries fed by volcanic headwaters and springs.

Compared to a straight or meandering river, a serpentine river creates exponentially more acres of riverbank for insects, fish, and amphibians. More shoreline equals more life. Snaky rivers create prime fish habitat in the undercut ledges at every outside bend and where two rivers converge. Additional habitat is created when tree limbs end up wedged at the outside of a bend. Serpentine rivers also form oxbows, or U-shaped sections of river that break away from the main course to form small, semi-isolated wetlands often used as nurseries for fish and amphibians. Hunters would consider the U-shaped area inside a sharp riverbend a perfect place to corral, kill, butcher, and clean a herd of prey. While many ancient cultures prohibited hunting sacred birds, there were many other bird species to hunt, and eggs to eat. Finally, because rivers silt up and freeze, a year-round spring is typically found near settlements.

Archaeological evidence has typically been found inside the sharp bend of a river, at a converging tributary, and/or on a high plateau overlooking the entire river system. The high elevation provided long views and the river was a natural barrier. Our distant ancestors hopped across Eurasia from one volcanic area to the next, always taking a particular interest in the hard and durable stones that are the byproduct of magmatism. In the shifting riverbeds and terraces that drain the headwaters of volcanic mountains were refractive rock crystals and other precious stones. Spear points and cutting tools made from obsidian and flint kept hominins near the top of the food chain, and protected them from hungry tigers, bears or wolfpacks.

Between 5.6 million and 2.5 million years ago, the earliest human-like species made the oldest stone artifacts ever found by the serpentine Middle Awash River in the volcanic mountains of central Ethiopia, where two bird flyways overlap. Discoveries included three species of *Australopithecus*, two of *Ardipithecus*, *Homo erectus,* and 12 *Homo sapiens* estimated to be about 157,000 years old. Another 30 settlement sites ranging in age from 1.7 million to 200,000 years old were found nearby at Melka Kunture in the Upper Awash Valley, where archaeologists discovered fossil remains of *Homo erectus* and *Homo sapiens.* Tens of thousands of blades and cores at Melka Kunture were mined from a massive outcrop of obsidian. In 1959, archaeologist Mary Leakey was working at Olduvai Gorge in a volcanic region of Tanzania where two bird flyways overlap when she discovered a skull belonging to a 3.2-million-year-old hominin she named Lucy. Since then, archaeologists have identified 60 different hominin types at Olduvai Gorge, known as the "Cradle of Mankind."

Homo erectus and the First Road Trip

Emerging about two million years ago, Homo erectus was more than a foot taller than previous primates, and its brain was 50 percent larger. Less hair meant more efficient perspiration, allowing for daytime travel over open terrain. Also critical to road-tripping were arched feet and a new balancing organ in the inner ear, allowing *Homo erectus* to walk or run while keeping its eyes trained on a distant target. A series of volcanic eruptions in East Africa between 1.8 and 2 million years ago may have given these distant ancestors a good reason to hit the road. In any case, *Homo erectus* was the first long-range trekker, spreading viable populations across Africa, the Near East, Europe, and Asia over two million years, and evolving into various sub-species along the way. When *Homo erectus* arrived in the volcanic Fertile Crescent and the Caucasus Mountains nearly two million years ago the entire region was an ecosystem on steroids, producing wild grains, fruits and nuts, and supporting every swimming, crawling, and flying creature imaginable.

About 1.5 million years ago, *Homo erectus* used hand axes to butcher hippos and wild cows at Ubeidiya, between the serpentine Jordan River and a converging tributary less than two miles south of the Sea of Galilee. Ubeidiya is located in the only active volcanic region of Israel, a country that ranks first in the world with 500 million migratory birds passing through each year. The extreme migratory bird population is due to Israel's location at the junction of three continents and the convergence of two heavily travelled bird flyways.

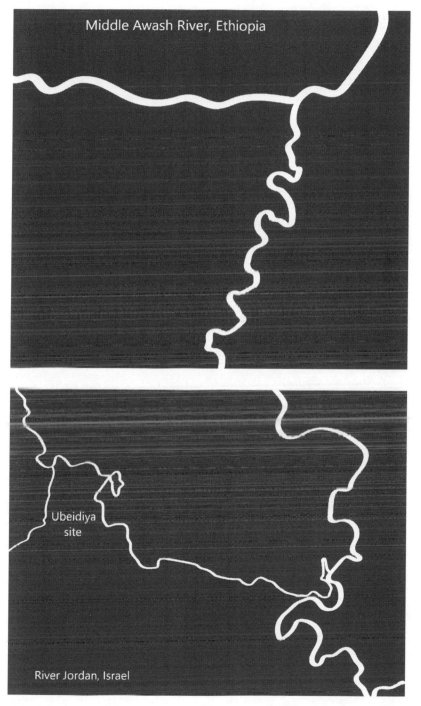

Middle Awash River, Ethiopia

Ubeidiya site

River Jordan, Israel

The largest single group of *Homo erectus* fossils on record was found in the Caucasus Mountains, an active volcanic region where three bird flyways converge. The fossils were found near Dmanisi, Georgia in the Mashavera River Valley, which drains the Javakheti volcanic chain to the west of the site. The occupation of the area began after more than 300 feet of lava had formed the Mashavera Basalt that dammed the Pinezaouri Valley, creating a lake. Dated between 1.75 and 1.8 million years old, the fossils were found on a promontory about 260 feet above the confluence of the Mashavera and Pinezaouri river valleys. Classified as *Homo erectus georgicus*, they stood about four feet tall, had small brains, canine teeth, and held their palms facing forward, but had relatively long legs and arched feet. One of the skeletons was an older man with a deteriorated jaw and no teeth who must have been helped to survive over a long period of time. Evidence of *Homo erectus* making obsidian tools 1.4 million years ago was found at nearby Mount Arteni in the Caucasus Mountains of Armenia, also where three bird flyways converge.

While a sustainable population of *Homo erectus* remained in the Near East until about 200,000 years ago, others kept going to India, where 1.5-million-year-old tools were found at Attirampakkam, a prehistoric site in the Kortallayar River basin in Tamil Nadu. Located where two flyways converge in the only active volcanic region in India, the site was also occupied about 385,000 years ago by unknown hominins. The only fossilized remains of *Homo erectus* found in India were estimated to be 550,000 years old, discovered near the village of Hathnora in the Narmada rift valley of Central India. The rift is part of the Deccan Traps, one of the largest volcanic features on earth, created 66 million years ago by upwarping tectonic plates spewing lava over an area the size of Colorado and Nevada combined. The basaltic layer is more than 6,600 feet deep. Just north of the Narmada River in the foothills of the Vindhya Range are 750 rock shelters, some of which were occupied more than 100,000 years ago.

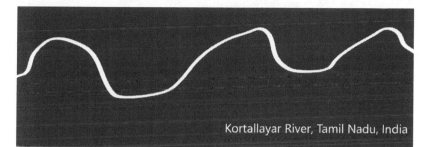

Kortallayar River, Tamil Nadu, India

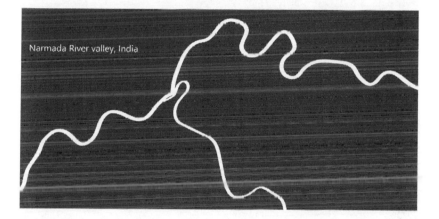

Narmada River valley, India

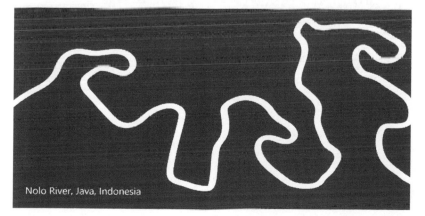

Nolo River, Java, Indonesia

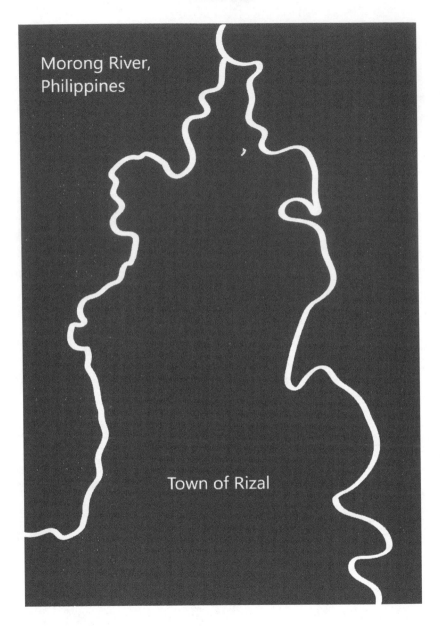

Morong River, Philippines

Town of Rizal

Sustainable populations of *Homo erectus* reached Indonesia, the Philippines, and northeast China. Archaeologists confirmed in 2014 that it was probably *Homo erectus* who used stone tools to slaughter rhinoceros and small elephants about 709,000 years ago near the town of Rizal, in the volcanic Philippines. A recent study concluded that *Homo erectus* built boats to establish a viable population on the island of Java 1.8 million years ago. A 500,000-year-old freshwater shell with zig-zag markings was found along the Solo River on Java, making it the oldest hominin engraving to date. In much later ancient human cultures, including the Celts and ancient Egyptians, the zig-zag symbol stood for water or river.

Neanderthals, Volcanos & Sacred Birds

Three Neanderthal teenagers left more than 50 footprints in rain-softened pyroclastic ash and mud about 350,000 years ago on the slopes of the Roccamonfina volcano in southern Italy. One took a switchback route down the slope, another went straight, and the third took a wider, curved path. Archaeologists determined the footprints were left soon after a volcanic eruption, so soon that the trio may have witnessed it from afar. A later study determined the teenagers' route was connected to a regular Neanderthal travel corridor through the area.

The highest concentration of Neanderthal remains in France was found in the only active volcanic region in the country, in the southwest. The only active volcanic region in Germany also coincides with a cluster of Neanderthal sites. In Spain the only volcanic area is on the northeast coast of the Mediterranean and coincides with a major Neanderthal settlement at Serinyà Prehistoric Cave Park in Banyoles. The volcanic areas in Spain, France, Italy, and Germany are overflown by the same two global bird flyways. Neanderthal settlements in Israel only appear in the single volcanic region of that country, southwest of the Sea of Galilee, where two bird flyways converge in a narrow north-south corridor.

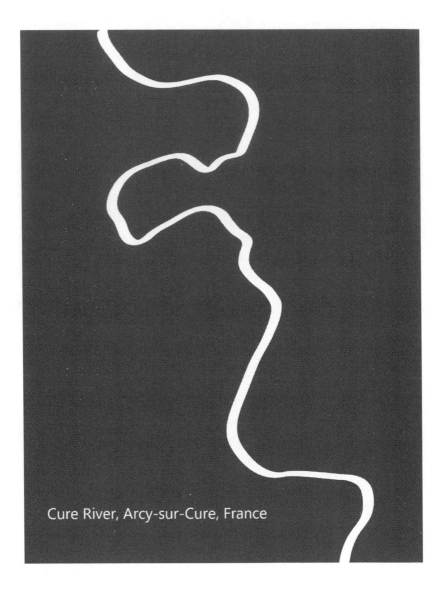

Cure River, Arcy-sur-Cure, France

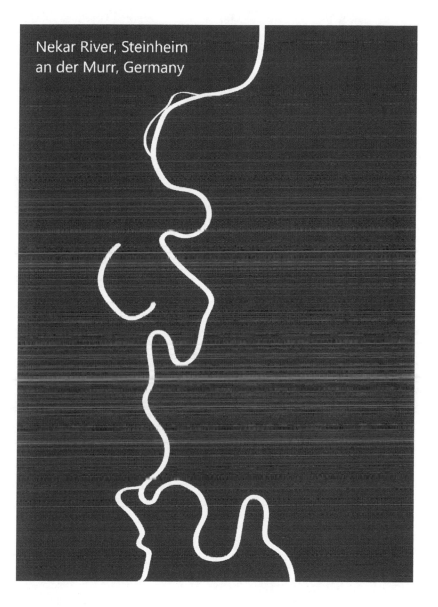

Nekar River, Steinheim
an der Murr, Germany

Piles of wing bones and talons found in caves across Europe in the last decade have revealed that Neanderthals had a very special relationship with birds. A 2010 study published in the journal *PNAS* concluded that Neanderthals plucked the feathers of raptors at Fumane Cave in northern Italy, probably to be used as ritual ornaments in "the social and symbolic sphere..." Of the 22 bird species found buried in Fumane Cave, the most common were black vultures, golden eagles, and red-footed falcons. Curiously, all the wing bones were gathered in a pile against the east wall of the cave. In a similar case, Neanderthals buried only the wing bones of crows in Cova Negra cave in southeastern Spain.

A study described in Clive Finlayson's 2019 book *The Smart Neanderthal* concluded that Neanderthals carefully removed wing feathers mostly from golden eagles, white-tailed eagles, bearded vultures, Eurasian black vultures, and ravens. Finlayson concluded that Neanderthals perceived certain birds as sacred and used feathers as symbolic ornaments to perform rituals. Finlayson noted a "growing body of data that demonstrates the appearance of modern behavior in extinct [Neanderthal] populations of Europe, well before the immigration of humans." At the Zaskalnaya VI site in Crimea, a Neanderthal made seven equidistant notches on a raven bone about 40,000 years ago, which some archaeologists believe were made for symbolic purposes.

In caves from Spain to France, Italy, and Croatia, archaeologists believe Neanderthals carefully removed the talons from dead birds, mostly from the rare imperial eagle. The study identified 10 sites where Neanderthals removed talons, all located in a swath of territory where the East Atlantic and Mediterranean/Black Sea flyways converge. In one outlying case, Neanderthals buried the webbed feet of a whooper swan at Baume de Gigny cave in southeastern France. Although physical evidence is elusive, many scholars believe the talons were worn around the neck, a practice found in later indigenous cultures. A study published in

Science Advances in 2019 argued that if Neanderthals wore talons as ornaments, it means they "had social and cultural structures complex enough to convey the use and meaning of [the talons] both in time, from generation to generation, and through space. This represents a remarkable advance with respect to our knowledge about the symbolic behavior of the Neanderthals..." The study added that later human cultures "have used raptor claws/talon for the elaboration of a great variety of elements associated with rituals, dances, personal adornments, grave goods, etc."

Guess Who's Coming to Dinner?

For more than 150 years western culture made a caricature of Neanderthals, depicting them as apelike, stupid, and brutish. For those not keeping up with taxonomic journals, the joke's on us. It turns out we're the same species, reunited by genetic science as long-lost brothers and sisters. We're *Homo sapiens sapiens* and they're *Homo sapiens neanderthalensis*. During the past decade, genetic evidence has confirmed beyond a doubt the two subspecies interbred extensively from Europe to Asia over a period of at least 30,000 years and possibly much longer.

Our growing family may soon officially welcome a mysterious third interbreeding member, currently known only as Denisovans. Fossil evidence of this long-lost cousin was discovered in a cave in the Altai Mountains of Russia, including a finger estimated to be 41,000 years old and a molar dating back 227,000 years. Denisova Cave overlooks the serpentine Anui River where three flyways converge (East Asia/East Africa, Central Asia, and East Asia/Australasia). A route of the East Asia/East Africa Flyway runs directly northeast from the Horn of Africa to the Altai Mountains.

Denisovans were tall with large skulls and lived comfortably in high mountain ranges due to a gene that regulates blood hemoglobin. In 2014, a University of California study found the hemoglobin gene was passed from Denisovans to Tibetans. Heading south from the Altai Mountains, two bird migration routes reach Tibet, where the only Denisovan DNA found outside the Altai Mountains was discovered in sediments excavated from Baishiya Karst Cave, located at an altitude of 10,500 feet. The cave's vantage point allowed the occupants to scan the entire landscape. A Lanzhou University study published in the October 2020 issue of *Science* found that Denisovans built fires in Baishiya Karst Cave about 100,000 years ago, again about 60,000 years ago, and possibly for a third phase about 45,000 years ago.

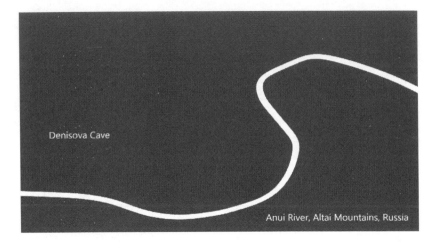

If Denisovans are found to be another *Homo sapiens* subspecies, scientists have already picked out a name: *Homo sapiens denisova*, the name, perhaps unfortunately, deriving from a hermit named Denis who once lived in the Altai Mountains cave where the first fossil evidence was found. Among the criteria scientists will consider when deciding if Denisovans are a third *Homo sapiens* subspecies are genetic studies confirming that Neanderthals, Denisovans, and modern humans all had sex and bore hybrid children as recently as 40,000 years ago in the Altai Mountains of Central Asia.

A 2018 study by the University of Oxford found the

interbreeding at Denisova Cave began much earlier when "Denny" was born about 95,000 years ago to a Neanderthal mother and a Denisovan father. "Denny" is not only the first direct hominin hybrid ever found, but one of his Denisovan father's ancestors was a Neanderthal: the original blended family. Geneticists have also found unknown "archaic" DNA in the Denisovan genome, which is suspected to be the result of ancient interbreeding with an Asian form of *Homo erectus*. Up to five percent of the genome of indigenous people living today in Australia, the Solomon Islands, part of the Philippines, and Papua New Guinea was inherited from Denisovans, almost twice as much as the 2.6 percent of DNA inherited from Neanderthals by western Europeans.

Just a decade ago, many scholars argued against the idea that humans ever interbred with Neanderthals. Now there's conclusive evidence that humans and Neanderthals engaged in coitus over a period of at least 30,000 years, mostly in the Near East but also in Asia, where they also had sexual intercourse with Denisovans. There's no evidence of violence, only sex, and geneticists continue to discover the true extent of the intercontinental romp. In terms of mixing DNA, the more than agreeable relations between the three subspecies were indisputably a major factor in *Homo sapiens sapiens* becoming the robust and successful specimen it is today.

Questions abound. How exactly did the three sub-species meet? Why did they all get along so famously? A 2013 study published in *Current Anthropology* estimated the total Neanderthal population at any one time was between 5,000 and 70,000. Scholars estimate the population of early *Homo sapiens* may have reached 30,000, but dramatically dropped to as few as 1,000 about 70,000 years ago. Considering the sparse evidence of Denisovans, no one has offered a reliable population estimate. With three populations spread over the continents of Africa, Europe, and Asia, how did they all end up having sex in a cave in the Altai Mountains? How did they find each other? What was the attraction? The perplexing questions begin to resolve themselves if all hominins routinely traveled on the same bird migration routes through the same volcanic regions. If the trio of sub-species crossed paths because of their shared belief in the wisdom of following birds, it would have been relatively easy to establish common ground. Maybe one group wore feathers in their hair while another wore eagle-talon necklaces. Perhaps they both carried obsidian or quartz artifacts. Maybe the languages they spoke were different but were all based in birdsong.

The Church of Birds & Serpents

The image of hundreds of thousands of birds flocking over a landscape of serpent-shaped rivers echoes clearly in cross-cultural creation myths.

In nature religions, the world tree often appears in creation stories as the axis or center of the world where birds perch in the highest branches with a serpent living at the base, symbolizing the snaky curves of creeks and rivers. In the American Midwest, the Menominee and Ho-Chunk tribes described a great serpent creating the winding river passage known as the Wisconsin Dells by wriggling downstream from its home near a big lake. Birds and serpents were polar opposite, representing two halves of a dualistic universe of upper and lower, hot and cold, light and dark. Creation stories from Greece to India, China, and the Americas describe a divine bird mating with a serpent or dragon to produce people. The miracle of creation occurred where birds and serpents met.

After the Greek goddess Eurynome emerged naked from the primordial waves, the serpent Ophion made love to her and she became a bird who hatched a universal egg, from which came a myriad of creatures. In Hindu legend, Kasyapa's wife Vinata gave birth to the Garuda bird while his other wife Kadru gave birth to a thousand little snakes. The Vietnamese creation story describes the goddess An Co flying down from the sky, mating with a dragon prince, and producing a sack of eggs that hatched into humans. In ancient China, the Phoenix was the ancestor of all birds, and a pair of dragons were the ancestors of all other creatures. In Guatemala a Kekchi king killed his daughter after she became pregnant by a hummingbird, but her blood became dozens of small snakes that incubated in a bottle and became women. What appear to be bizarre mythical stories of inter-species mating may have been a symbolic map of the environment where our most distant ancestors first emerged.

To the Americas

The closest known genetic relatives of Native Americans lived at least 14,000 years ago where three flyways converge in the volcanic region of Ust-Kyakhta in southern Russia, on the northern border of Mongolia, according to a 2020 genetic study by the Max Planck Institute.

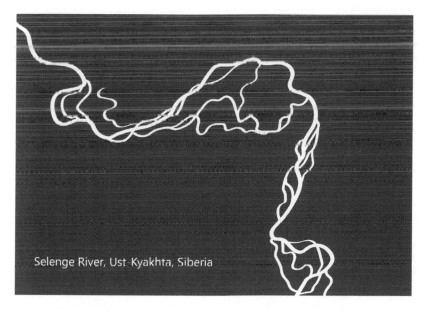

Selenge River, Ust-Kyakhta, Siberia

For more than a century, scholars believed human migration to the Americas occurred about 13,000 years ago, across a land bridge from Siberia to Alaska. But over the last 20 years archaeologists discovered far older settlement sites throughout the Americas, and the old theory fell apart. Most scientists have now accepted the Coastal Migration Hypothesis, first outlined in a 2007 study, which concluded that about 16,000 years ago Asian mariners could have used small boats to follow a kelp forest that tracked east near the southern coast of the glacial icepack to the Aleutian Islands, Alaska, and down the Pacific coastline of the Americas. The study found the kelp forest and the sea life it attracted would have produced enough food to sustain a viable group of mariners. Beneath the kelp forest the Pacific Ring of Fire supplies the oceanic vegetation with minerals along its entire route. The study didn't mention the active boundaries of two global bird flyways that also track with the kelp forest, supplying it from above with nutrient-rich droppings released by tens of millions of waterfowl.

By orders of magnitude, the sky was filled with a far greater number of birds 16,000 years ago, a time when it was common wisdom that birds carried the seeds of vegetation. The Asian mariners would have been encouraged to see a kelp forest spread out below a busy bird migration route disappearing beyond the horizon of the ocean. Perhaps it was the combination of the kelp forest and bird flyways that inspired them to take the overseas adventure. It's plausible the mariners believed the souls of their ancestors were inside the migrating birds and could be trusted to guide them.

Numerous tribes in California and the Pacific Northwest believed birds carried the souls of their ancestors. On Vancouver Island, Kwakiutl dancers manipulated strings to open an eagle-head "Transformation Mask," revealing the painted mask of a human ancestor inside the eagle-head.

The Serrano and Shoshoni of southern California say their ancestors came from the north, following an eagle to the San Bernardino Mountains, where the tribes settled. The Mojave of California and Arizona and the Apache of Arizona and New Mexico say their ancestors followed a hummingbird into this world by climbing a vine through a hole.

In Arizona, the Tohono O'odham once practiced singing treks, following the directions outlined in the verses of The Oriole Song, which guided them to dozens of sacred springs, caves, and mountains. The O'odham believed their singers learned the melodies of the travel song from birds that appeared in their dreams. Archaeologists have identified some of the ancient trails, and in March 2015 a group of O'odham men revived the ancient practice, making a 286-mile trek from southwest Arizona through lava fields and dunes to the sacred salt flats along the Gulf of California, and back. The last verse of the Oriole Song conveys the sense of a journey's end.

The songs are ending as they go their separate ways,
from the center of our songs,
the wind comes, flowing back and forth,
erasing the tracks of the people,
ready to place them here again.

In Mexico, the Aztecs believed they were led from their northern homeland of Aztlan (Land of the Herons) by the sun god Huitzilopochtli, also known as the Hummingbird of the Left. Legend has it that Montezuma sent a search party north to find the mythic Aztlan. When the search party came to the mountain birthplace of the sun god, he suddenly appeared and turned them into birds for the last leg of the voyage.

Volcano-Hopping in the Americas

In the American West, the Pacific and Central Americas flyways overlap in active volcanic areas of northern Texas, the Southwest, and parts north to Idaho, including most of the oldest Native American settlements in the region. The converging flyways encompass Coopers Ferry, Idaho (16,000 years ago), the Clovis culture of New Mexico (13,300 years ago), the Buttermilk Creek Complex in Salado, Texas (15,500 years ago), the Hohokam homeland in Arizona (4,000 years ago), the Anasazi/Pueblo cultures of the Four Corners region (2,000 years ago), and the Fremont of Utah (1,400 years ago). In 2021, archaeologists announced the oldest evidence of humans in the Americas: a set of 23,000-year-old footprints preserved in White Sands National Park in New Mexico, also where two flyways overlap in an active volcanic region.

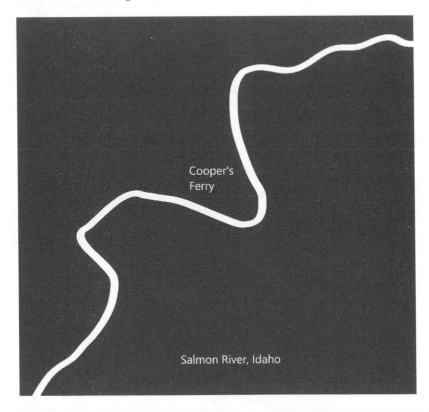

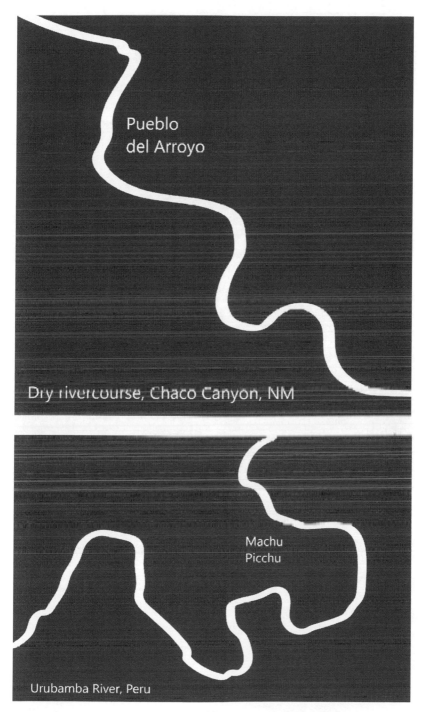

Pueblo del Arroyo

Dry rivercourse, Chaco Canyon, NM

Machu Picchu

Urubamba River, Peru

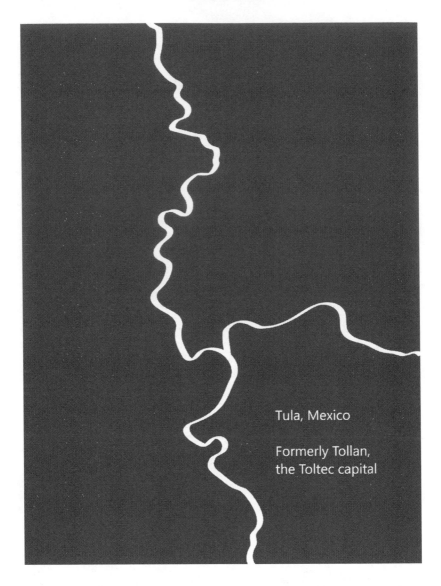

Tula, Mexico

Formerly Tollan,
the Toltec capital

In Mexico and Central America, the Aztec and Maya settled in regions where three bird flyways converge in volcanic areas, including El Mirador in southeastern Mexico, a massive Mayan metropolis recently discovered by LIDAR technology and estimated to be more than 3,000 years old, rolling back the clock on the Mayan civilization by a thousand years. Between 1,000 and 800 years ago in central Mexico, where three global flyways converge in a volcanic region, the Toltec people celebrated their feathered-serpent creator god Quetzalcoatl in the capital city of Tollán, known as "Place of the Reeds." At creation, Quetzalcoatl mixed its quetzal bird blood with its rattlesnake blood and applied it to the bones of pre-human ancestors to create human beings. The city of Tollán was known for its temples, pools, gardens, and civic spaces; its artisans were known for their beautiful works of obsidian.

After the Toltec decline, Aztec legend recounts a trek when a priest had a vision of an island in a lake with an eagle perched on a cactus, tearing apart and devouring a snake. The next day the travelers came upon a lake with an island in the middle where it was said the priest's vision came true before their eyes. The lake became the city of Tenochtitlán, the cactus became the Aztec world tree, and the feathered serpent was worshipped as the creator. Given the timeline and shared beliefs, it's plausible that when the city of Tollán went into decline, a sub-group of Toltec migrated southeast 60 miles to build the lake city and morph into the Aztec. In any case, the Aztec put their engineering genius to work at Tenochtitlán, building causeways that connected dozens of island-neighborhoods. In the lake, farmers created islands up to a hundred feet in diameter and staked them to the bottom. Maximizing the shorelines at Tenochtitlan was likely an intentional effort to further contribute to the bountiful ecosystem, where three global flyways converge.

When a Spanish missionary asked the Aztec about the Toltec, the Aztec offered high praise for the birds in the city of Tollán, saying "there dwelt all varieties of birds of precious feather: the lovely cotinga, the resplendent trogon, the touripal, the roseate spoonbill," according to the Florentine Codex. When the conquistador Hernán Cortés wrote his second letter from New Spain to the Spanish king in 1522, he noted an entire street in Tenochtitlán set aside for gamebirds, including "partridges, quails, wild ducks, fly-catchers, widgeons, turtle-doves, pigeons, reedbirds, parrots, sparrows, eagles, hawks, owls, and kestrels; they sell likewise the skins of some birds of prey, with their feathers, head, beak, and claws." Regardless of Cortes' glowing account the Spanish later destroyed much of the city, and ultimately the lake was drained. The ruins of Tenochtitlán are now buried under Mexico City.

In South America, two bird flyways converge in a relatively narrow corridor at high altitudes in volcanic regions of the Andes Mountains, including Machu Picchu, Lake Titicaca, and the city of Cusco, the oldest city in the Americas, founded in 1100. Obsidian artifacts are found at archaeological sites up and down the Pacific Coast of the Americas.

Although there's no active volcanic areas in the eastern U.S., the highest concentration of Native American mounds in the country is found in a north-south corridor where the Central and Atlantic Americas flyways converge from the Great Lakes to the Gulf Coast. The mounds were built by the Adena and Hopewell farming cultures of Ohio and dozens of tribes that fall under the category of Mississippian cultures.

Clay headpots crafted 1,000 years ago by Mississippian cultures depicted the heads of infants, juveniles, and adults, and have been found in burials of all ages and both sexes. The decorations on the headpots represent an upper world of birds, a middle world of humans, animals, and vegetation, and a lower world of serpents, according to archaeologist Bretton T. Giles of Kansas State University, who authored a chapter in the book, *New Methods and Theories for Analyzing Mississippian Imagery,* published in 2021. Giles noted that the bird and serpent symbols on the headpots were consistent with a map of the cosmos created by the Osage of Kansas. In addition to their belief that the redbird gave them the gift of language, the Osage made headdresses from swan skins and woodpecker beaks, and used a pipe covered in the feathers of different birds during peace ceremonies with other tribes.

Eco-History and Religion

Following migratory birds through volcanic regions, our distant ancestors discovered streambeds littered with colorful rock crystals and shiny volcanic glass they made into spearpoints and blades. It's impossible to know when the foundations of a cosmology of the universe were first laid, but it probably occurred long before *Homo sapiens* emerged more than 300,000 years ago. It appears early humans inherited an eco-history filled with a wide variety and high population of birds, serpentine creeks and rivers, active volcanos, mountain springs and precious stones, all progenitors of mythic themes that would weave their way through ancient myth and religious history, establishing near-universal symbols such as the cosmic egg, the world tree, and the celestial pole.

Chapter 3

The Divinity of Eco-Farming

More than 13,000 years ago an unknown tribe burned and cleared land in a volcanic area of Central America where three global bird flyways converge. The intentional burning occurred at Lake La Yeguada in Panama, more than 3,000 years before the first domesticated seeds were planted in the region. The burning and clearing may have been intended to create open fields of rich, volcanic soil below a superhighway of bird migration. Considering the divinity of seed-bearing birds in ancient cultures, it's plausible that Lake La Yeguada was a sacred site attended by a priesthood of eco-farmers. It's plausible that drums were played, songs were sung, and dancers danced as the waves of migratory birds arrived in the spring.

In western scholarship it was long believed that farming developed as a necessity in areas lacking food resources. Modern archaeology has shown the opposite to be true. Crop farming typically began where two or three bird flyways converge in fertile volcanic areas, and more specifically along serpentine rivers where tributaries converged, the same bountiful ecosystems where hominins had been gathering wild plants, fruits, and nuts for untold millennia. In the only volcanic region of Israel southwest of the Sea of Galilee there's clear evidence of people intensively harvesting wild plants 23,000 years ago, about 11,000 years before crop production began in the same region.

In creation legends across the globe, birds were given credit for creating the landscape, delivering seeds to the soil, and tending to the most beautiful gardens on earth so they might grow in the sun's benevolent rays. Ultimately it was humanity's turn to form the landscape and plant the seeds of vegetation. It's plausible that early farmers perceived their own re-shaping of the landscape and planting of seeds as sacred re-enactments of original divine acts carried out by migratory birds. In volcanic regions of eastern Turkey and northern Syria, the farming villages of Abu Hureyra and Nevalı Çori developed about 12,000 years ago where the East Asia/East Africa Flyway converges with the Mediterranean/Black Sea Flyway. In the Americas, the Pacific and Central Americas flyways converge on the volcanic southwest coast of Ecuador, where archaeologists believe farmers domesticated melons 11,840 years ago. Mythological evidence across numerous farming cultures supports the notion that migratory birds were divine partners in agriculture.

The Sumerian Garden of Eden

Written on clay tablets about 5,000 years ago, a Sumerian creation story identified the Garden of Eden as a lava field high on a mountain where an ark full of animals landed after a catastrophic flood, where bird-gods first taught the Sumerians how to farm.

After the glacial ice sheets of northern Europe began to melt about 14,700 years ago, the North Atlantic rose as much as 72 feet over the next three millennia. About 12,000 years ago the North American ice sheet suddenly melted into the North Atlantic, and the Mediterranean Sea surged north into a freshwater lake that swiftly became the Black Sea. People living in the Near East at the time had endured almost 3,000 years of continually rising oceans and widespread flooding from the melting of regional icecaps. There was no reason to believe that sea levels would stop rising, and every reason to believe the climate chaos would continue, including dramatic temperature shifts that disrupted food sources. Nature was once a consistent provider, but that was changing fast, and humanity went looking for more reliable sources of nourishment.

Far from the flooded shorelines, early Sumerians headed into the thawing highlands of eastern Turkey and northern

Syria. It was time to shape Mother Nature into a source of sustenance, time for the plow and the hoe. The Sumerians ultimately established a vast farming empire along the Tigris and Euphrates in southern Mesopotamia, becoming the first civilization to invent a form of writing. Their creation story featuring the supreme twin gods Enlil and Enki, often depicted with large wings. Enlil was a storm god who commanded the air and wind. Enki was the god of water, magic, and wisdom, and was responsible for good harvests. The story begins with lesser winged gods known as Annunaki complaining they were tired of tending the gardens of earth, inspiring Enki to create a totally new creature that would take over the job. But after Enki created the first humans, his brother Enlil was annoyed with all the noise they made and decided to destroy them with a flood.

Having a soft spot for his creation, Enki warned a virtuous man and his family of the coming deluge, urging them to gather all the animals and build an ark. After the flood receded, the ark landed on a high lava plain, a landscape known in the Sumerian language as an "edin." Enki taught the survivors of the flood to cultivate the rich basaltic soil, as reflected in Sumerian verses describing the virtues of a small beak-like pickax, which kills "bad" plants while tending to others. The ark itself was packed with surprisingly well-behaved wild animals, likely an idealized symbol of early Sumerian pastoral farming. In the end, Enlil and Enki succeeded in taking the burden of maintaining the gardens of earth away from the lesser gods and passing it on to humans. Meanwhile, Enki felt sorry for the toil that humans faced, so he sent healing plants to alleviate suffering, and as God of the arts he sent emissaries to teach people how to sing and dance.

Karaca Dağ: A Volcanic Nursery?

Adventurers and documentary producers have long focused on Turkey's volcanic Mt. Ararat as the site where Noah's ark landed after the flood. In contrast there's been little interest in identifying the landing place of the Sumerian ark, despite an impressive chain of evidence pointing to the shield volcano Karaca Dağ in southwestern Turkey.

In 2006, the Max Planck Institute for Plant Breeding Research discovered that the genetically common ancestor of 68 contemporary types of cereal still grow as wild plants on Karaca Dağ, suggesting it could be the original source of domesticated plants in the Near East. Just 60 miles south of Karaca Dağ is the 11,500-year-old temple at Göbekli Tepe featuring a wide variety of animals etched in stone, suggesting it was intended to commemorate the nearby landing of the Sumerian ark. Less than 150 miles south of Göbekli Tepe is Abu Hureyra, the oldest farming village on record, dating back 12,000 years. Perhaps the slopes of Karaca Dağ were a sacred garden where early farmers gathered wild cereals to domesticate at early farming settlements in the area such as Abu Hureyra, Nevalı Çori, and Çayönü.

In the Sumerian Epic of Gilgamesh, the hero travels to a jeweled garden of the gods on Mt. Mashu, where the peaks reach the heavens, and the depths lead to the underworld. Described as covered in cedar trees, Mt. Mashu was said to be the source of four rivers. Once known as Mount Masia, the volcanic Karaca Dağ towers over the landscape at 6,419 feet. Its depths have been volcanically active on and off for more than three million years. The jewels identified by Gilgamesh may have been rock crystals with large facets that naturally occur in basaltic soil, sparkling in the sun like gems. Satellite mapping shows up to six or seven rivers running from Karaca Dağ, a condition that typically changes over time. Cedars once grew in abundance south of the Black Sea, though only a small population remains.

Demeter and Persephone

In ancient Greek myth a young woman is taken to the Underworld for six months each winter, where she eats pomegranates, a fruit that is visibly full of seeds. Her mother remains in Greece and worries about her daughter, who returns every year with pomegranate seeds amid the blooms of spring.

The young woman was the goddess Persephone and her mother was Demeter, the goddess of agriculture. The plot suggests the goddess Persephone was intended to embody migratory birds, which deliver seeds when they arrive in spring, a theory supported by direct physical evidence. At least four temples dedicated to Demeter and Persephone were built at sites where flocks of migratory birds still take off or make landfall today, according to BirdLife International's global flyway maps. One temple to Demeter and Persephone is on the Greek island of Naxos, where birds follow a route of the Mediterranean/ Black Sea Flyway on their southward migration. After crossing the sea, the route makes landfall at the ancient city of Cyrene in Libya, where there's another temple to the pair of farming goddesses. Cyrene was built on the highest ground in the region and was known for its fertile soil and lush plant life. The mythic bird-women known as Seirenes, who lured sailors astray, were depicted in ancient art as the handmaidens of Persephone.

A third temple to the goddesses was built in Syracuse on the island of Sicily, a stopover site on the Mediterranean/Black Sea Flyway for birds flying from Italy to North Africa. After taking off from Sicily a route of the flyway makes landfall at the ancient city of Carthage, where a fourth temple to Demeter and Persephone was built. During the Siege of Syracuse, warriors from Carthage lost the battle but sacked the temple to Demeter and Persephone. They later thought better of wrecking the sacred structure and built their own temple to the agricultural goddesses back home in Carthage. All four temples were built between 2,700 and 2,350 years ago.

The link between Persephone and migratory birds is new information in western scholarship, which has long debated the meaning behind the myth of Demeter and Persephone and the related Eleusinian Mysteries, including the annual processional trek from Athens to Eleusis. Perhaps the procession was a re-enactment of bird migration, concluding with ritual offerings to ensure success for migratory birds crossing the sea.

About 700 miles west of Cyrene on the coast of North Africa was the ancient city of Leptis Magna, established by the Phoenicians about 2,650 years ago and located at another landfall on the Mediterranean/Black Sea Flyway. Due to the unusual fertility of its extensive olive groves, Leptis Magna was one of the biggest producers of olive oil in the Mediterranean region, its wealth paying for a large open temple and civic gathering place overlooking Port Livius. The city even minted its own coins and was able to remain independent under both the Carthaginian and Roman empires. The area remains an island of biodiversity today, according to Conservation International. A similar story unfolded at about the same time in eastern Sudan, where the Kush Empire emerged about 2,700 years ago in a modest and remote volcanic area where a major tributary enters the Nile, and two bird flyways converge. The empire's farming success built the opulent capital city of Meroe and more than 100 pyramids nearby. The Kush Empire rivaled the ancient Egyptians for more than a thousand years.

The Chinese Phoenix

In Chinese legend, Shennong the Flame Emperor led his people on a search for the best seed grain, traveling over hills, mountains, and rivers. Finally, a phoenix carrying grass in its beak appeared from above, and "a fine rain of glistening golden grain fell to earth at a sunlit spot not far away." When the people ran to the spot, they found a field of tender green shoots.

The roots of Chinese agriculture in the north and northwest are in rich loess soils, made up of wind-blown particulates of quartz, mica, and feldspar, all of which originate in volcanic rocks. One of the earliest farming areas was west of Beijing, where the Datong-Fengzen volcanic field features cinder cones reaching more than 5,000 feet above sea level. About 4,000 years ago, the semi-legendary Xie Dynasty emerged as a farming empire in the volcanic regions of the Shandong and Henan provinces, followed in the same area by the Shang Dynasty 400 years later, when the first Chinese music and writing was produced. About 2,000 years ago during the Han Dynasty, *The Annals of Wu and Yue* suggest a link between Yu the Great (emperor), birds, farming, and the gods of heaven. "Heaven praised Yu's virtue and rewarded his achievements by making the hundred birds return to work the marshes and fields on the behalf of people."

Burying Birds in the Americas

Native American farming cultures emerged in volcanic areas where the Pacific Americas and Central Americas flyways overlap in New Mexico, Arizona, Colorado, Utah, and Idaho. They also emerged in the Eastern Woodlands, a non-volcanic region east of the Mississippi River where the Central Americas and Atlantic Americas flyways converge. Archaeologists believe some of the Eastern Woodlands were burned and cleared to produce a diverse landscape.

About 1,300 years ago a small city specializing in maize production emerged on the Mississippi River just east of St. Louis. Given the name Cahokia by archaeologists, the urban trading center consisted of 120 large earthen mounds with a population of 20,000 or more. It was a place of seasonal feasts and the sacred theater of music and dance. At the center of the city was a serpentine tributary near a mound standing 100 feet tall, created from layers of past structures, buried ancestors, and fill. Now known as Monk's Mound, it's still almost 1,000 feet long and more than 800 feet wide. From above, the earth-worked edges of one end appear to be shaped like the tail feathers of a bird. Hundreds of small clay tablets were found in the area showing a birdman "falcon dancer" on one side and a tight triangular pattern on the other that may represent snakeskin.

The recent excavation of two mounds at Cahokia suggest that birds played a major role in sacred ceremonies. After analyzing the remains of 343 swans buried inside Mound 34, archaeologists found the swans were not eaten, but many of the wing bones were used to make beads and awls. Cahokia is just north of a modern-day trumpeter swan wintering ground, which may have been larger and could have encompassed the city when the first mounds were built.

A total of 25 bird species were found inside Mound 51, including bald eagles, red-tailed hawks, peregrine falcons, herons, pelicans, egrets, ravens, parakeets, woodpeckers and 13 kinds of ducks. Very few of the birds in the mound were eaten as food at the time, suggesting the burials were part of a religious ritual. In a 2010 report on the Cahokia excavation, archaeologist Lucretia S. Kelly referred to the Hidatsa of North Dakota, who believed three species of waterfowl delivered different varieties of seed in early spring: Geese carried maize, ducks delivered beans, and swans were associated with squash. Kelly wrote that the swan burials at Cahokia were also linked to squash seeds. Some archaeologists believe the Cahokia culture influenced the Adena farming culture, which began growing maize, beans, and squash in the Ohio River Valley about 1,000 years ago. Anthropologists believe the upper world of the Adena cosmology was ruled by Thunderbirds while the lower world was the realm of horned serpents. Among the artifacts the Adena left behind were wooden pipes carved in the shape of a birdman, not unlike the falcon dancer depicted on the clay tablets at Cahokia.

Feathered Dreadlocks & the
Seeds of Food Mountain

About 4,000 years ago in volcanic southern Arizona, the mound-building Hohokam started growing domestic maize, beans, squash, and pumpkins. Within 500 years, they were building extensive irrigation canals in the floodplain of the Santa Cruz

River. Hohokam men crafted obsidian tools, wore their hair in dreadlocks decorated with white feathers, and crafted turquoise mosaic pendants with a bird in the center.

In volcanic Mesoamerica, the Aztec feathered-serpent creator god Quetzalcoatl was shown *carrying a pointed hollow staff filled with seeds, or* with flowers coming out of its beak. Known as the teacher of farming, Quetzalcoatl turned into an ant to crawl inside Food Mountain and bring maize seeds to the people.

In northern Peru, human occupation of the Nanchoc Valley dates back 11,500 years, with evidence of domesticated squash being planted about 10,000 years ago at seasonal settlements where the Pacific and Central Americas flyways converge. The first pyramidal mounds were constructed about 4,000 years ago, celebrating agricultural themes. At the village of Aspero on the northern coast were more than a dozen large mounds, including one with a colorful arrangement of bird feathers buried at the top. At 10,335 feet in the Central Andes, the Tello Obelisk once stood in the middle of a circular plaza in front of *the Old Temple at Chavín de Huántar, built 2,850 years ago where the same two flyways overlap.* Carved in granite, one of the hardest rocks on earth, the obelisk showed a raptor dropping peanuts from the sky. A garden plaza was built across from the Old Temple featuring raised platforms that were once cultivated. The structures were built between two converging serpentine rivers.

Beneath the two flyways the ancient city of Tiwanaku was built at about 12,600 feet in a volcanic area of western Bolivia about 2,000 years ago. The megalithic Gate of the Sun features a birdman in the center attended on either side by three rows of birdmen. Around nearby Lake Titicaca, farmers reclaimed marshland by raising large mounds of mud, vegetation, and compost material where they grew potatoes, quinoa, and beans. The Incas took a similar approach in the volcanic mountains surrounding nearby Cusco, where at elevations between 12,500 and 16,400 feet, they grew potatoes and quinoa in raised fields covering more than 300 square miles.

Across cultures migratory birds were associated with the exotic seeds they brought from beyond the horizon every spring, just as the landscape came alive in grasses, flowers, and fruit trees. The symbolism of the seed was not far removed from the symbolism of the egg: Both were vessels that contained and protected the mysterious instructions by which life was created. While birds were closely linked with seeds, they were also universally linked with the creative power of the cosmic egg.

Chapter 4

The Cosmic Egg

Earth is an oblate spheroid, bulging out slightly around the middle. The distance from the center of the earth to the surface is 13 miles longer at the equator than at the poles. To a mountain climber at high altitude with a 360-degree view, the dome of the sky and the bowl of the earth appear somewhat ovate. The 1st century Chinese astronomer Chang Heng described the heavens as looking like "a hen's egg."

Myths of the cosmic egg are ancient and widespread, often featuring the same image: After the egg splits in two, one half forms the sky and the other becomes the earth. While the egg breaks in half, the two sides are not tossed into some cosmic compost. The symbolic language of myth has the two halves still fitting together, sky over earth. Perhaps jagged mountain ranges were like the broken edges of the eggshell. In many cosmic egg myths, the yolk becomes the sun. In Hindu mythology, a divine bird laid the egg of Brahma on the primordial waters, and at the heart of the egg was the sun. The aborigines of southwest Australia describe two kookaburra birds arguing in the dark before the sun existed. One bird threw the other's egg into the sky where the yolk burst into flames and became the sun.

Another category of cosmic egg myth tells of divine beings hatching from a cosmic egg and creating the world. In the Greek Orphic tradition, the hermaphroditic deity Phanes-Protogonus hatched from the Orphic Egg and created the other gods. In Slavic cultures the creator Rod hatched from a cosmic egg by the power of love, to create heaven and earth. After the Hindu god Purusa broke out of a cosmic egg, his skull formed the heavens, his breath became wind, and his blood became the seas. In Chinese myth, the giant P'an Ku hatched from a cosmic egg and pushed the two sides apart so the sun could shine down on the land. Like Purusa, his body parts transformed into the world around us.

The Original Cosmic Egg?

About 176,000 years ago, deep inside a cave in southern France, Neanderthals built small fires on an egg-shaped ring of stones while engaging in "some kind of symbolic or ritual behavior," according to a recent study by a team of 18 scientists.

After navigating 1,000 feet inside a subterranean complex and inching through narrow passages, local spelunkers discovered Bruniquel Cave and its archaeological remains in 1990. The cave is located in a volcanic region known as the "Capital of Prehistory," where 15 sites make up the highest concentration of Neanderthal habitation in the world. Reported in the May 2016 issue of *Nature*, the study concluded that Bruniquel Cave is the oldest known deep cave used for ritual behavior by Neanderthals, who heated and broke 124 stalagmites to create an oval ring 20 feet long and 14 feet across. Inside the oval was a circular stone ring, seven feet in diameter. The builders lit fires on parts of the structures, where remains of burnt animal bones were found. There were no signs of extended habitation, leading to the conclusion that the cave was used "for some kind of symbolic or ritual behavior." It's notable that building fires deep inside a mountain may have been an attempt to imitate and/or communicate with the fiery volcano gods.

Also in southern France, Neanderthals build twenty oval-shaped huts on the beach in modern-day Nice about 400,000 years ago, according to a 1960s study by the French archaeologist Henry de Lumley. Known as Terra Amata, the site yielded evidence that Neanderthals hunted red deer, wild cattle, and a small species of elephant, butchering them on the beach. In northern Iraq, eight oval-shaped hearths made of rock crystal were found near Neanderthal burials in Shanidar Cave. Taken together with widespread evidence that Neanderthals plucked feathers and removed talons from raptors for ceremonial purposes, it's plausible their core beliefs included something like a "cosmic egg."

In the southeast corner of the Serengeti Plain, in northern Tanzania, is the oldest structure in the archaeological record: An egg-shaped ring measuring 21 feet long and 15 feet across, with stone tools and bones inside the boundary. Located at Olduvai Gorge and estimated to be 1.9 million years old, archaeologists can't say who built the ring or what purpose it served. Although the measurements are nearly identical to the Neanderthal oval in Bruniquel Cave, it seems unlikely they were handed down orally over almost two million years. Perhaps in both cases the ring-makers were imitating eggs they observed in nature. The ratio of the short axis to the long axis in both cases is about 2/3, a match for eggs laid by pheasants, hens, ducks, turkeys, and other birds.

Oval Homes

For tens of thousands of years, people lived in round or oval structures intended to imitate the dome of the sky, often with a smoke-hole symbolically connecting to the heavens. Long before the development of agriculture and the advent of megalithic temples, each home was the equivalent of a sacred site.

The first oval homes built by humans in the archaeological record were constructed about 31,000 years ago at Dolni Vestonice in Moravia by the Gravettians, a name invented by scholars. Four thousand years later in nearby Predmost, the same culture built oval dwellings partly sunk into the ground and a large elliptical burial pit containing the remains of 20 people. The most well-known Gravettian artifact at Predmost is a figurine known as the Willendorf II Venus, featuring enormous ovate hips and egg-shaped belly. In ancient Moravia, the egg-shaped womb, oval homes, and an elliptical burial ground suggest the cosmic egg was at work throughout the cycle of life, reflecting deeply held beliefs about the cyclical and regenerative nature of the universe.

The Willendorf II Venus.

The people of the Near East lived in round or oval homes until about 10,500 years ago when pastoral farmers began building rectangular homes and sheep pens. While this fundamental change occurred first in the Near East, the same shift from round to square homes also took place when the indigenous farming cultures of the Americas developed on a large scale. Exactly what factors contributed to abandoning rounded homes in favor of square angles will likely remain a mystery, but the shift may be related to issues surrounding the sacredness of the female form.

It's generally accepted that circles and ovals are inherently symbolic of the female form, while the rectangular form is associated with the sharper angles of men. One thing is certain, the shift from circular to square houses in the Near East coincided with the beginning of a series of out-migrations to Europe. While the rectangular form of homes would persist for thousands of years in the male-dominated cultures of the Near East, the archaeological record shows the out-migrants who settled in Europe preferred rounded homes over the next 10,000 years, or until the Romans invaded. One of the oldest examples is the remains of ten oval-shaped huts estimated to be 9,000 years old, excavated in the 1970s at Mount Sandel, near Londonderry in Northern Ireland.

In the Americas, the Adena of Ohio lived in round homes when they emerged about 3,000 years ago, but when the Hopewell replaced them about 800 years later and intensified the development of agriculture, they built rectangular homes. But the Hopewell didn't abandon the oval shape entirely: The ceremonial Newark Earthworks site included a large ovate enclosure.

In southwestern Arizona about 4,000 years ago, the first Hohokam farmers lived in oval houses around an egg-shaped plaza. Even the enclosure set aside for trash was oval-shaped. About 350 years later the second phase of Hohokam culture built an extensive system of agricultural canals and favored square and rectangular homes. But the new Hohokam culture also included a massive building spree of about 200 oval depressions sunk into the earth, with the largest capable of holding 700 people. There is no archaeological consensus on the purpose of the structures. Some say the oval insets were ball-courts while others claim they were dance floors.

In the American Southwest, the traditional round shape of the earliest kivas and pit houses of the Ancestral Pueblo were replaced by the square and rectangular forms common in later Pueblo architecture, which also retained round forms in sacred contexts. About 1,500 years ago at Hovenweep, bordering Utah and Colorado, a group of farmers built partially sunken round homes and wore robes interwoven with domesticated turkey feathers. Rectangular shelters replaced the "pit houses" at Hovenweep 250 years later.

At Las Pircas in Chile, egg-shaped houses were built about 9,000 years ago at a time when farmers were still migratory, relying on small streams to supply modest irrigation systems. About 2,000 years later, canal-building made farming the primary source of food at Las Pircas, and oval homes were replaced with rectangular forms. Meanwhile, ancient burials along the northern coast of Peru were often in shallow ovoid pits, with the dead in a fetal position.

If farming began as a sacred practice of re-enacting the original role of birds in planting seeds at creation, it appears to have ultimately morphed into something more practical and mundane. It's not hard to imagine that a ritualized, sacred approach to every aspect of agricultural life would ultimately clash with the demands of efficiency and productivity, especially when feeding children was at stake. Compared to round forms, far less labor is needed to build rectangles, and squared-off spaces can be used more efficiently. Early farmers along the lower Yangtze River dug egg-shaped "puddle-fields" to cultivate rice about 6,000 years ago near modern-day Shanghai, but as agriculture developed, they switched to the rectangular fields that remain today. It appears that squared-off homes, barns, canals, and fields became utilitarian areas, while rounded structures remained sacred spaces.

The ovate form of the cosmic bird egg is found elsewhere

in nature. Early farmers grew plants from seeds that were mostly ovoid in shape. The coconut palm, almond, and hazel trees were all sacred trees producing oval-shaped nuts used to make nutritious milk across ancient cultures. The ovate leaves of the sacred Chinese white mulberry tree are transformed by silkworms into an oval cocoon. It appears the ovate form itself was perceived to be inherently infused with divine qualities.

Megalithic Eggs

As farming cultures developed, so did the construction of enormous stone monuments. Farming made its debut in the Near East about 12,000 years ago at Abu Hureyra in northern Syria, and just 500 years later construction began on the first megalithic structure in the archaeological record at nearby Göbekli Tepe, where people from villages 100 miles around gathered for annual festivals and feasts.

The burnt remains of thousands of animals, mostly wild cattle, were buried nearby and stone vats have yielded the ancient remains of mashing and malting. In parts of Western Europe, megaliths began to appear as farming developed about 5,000 to 6,000 years ago. In Korea, agriculture began about 5,500 years ago, and was soon followed by the erection of standing stones and dolmens. Early farmers built the massive Pueblos of Chaco Canyon. In northern Peru, the first megaliths appeared about 4,000 years ago, about the same time that migratory farmers were transforming seasonal settlements into year-round villages.

When the communal and semi-nomadic nature of the hunter-gathering culture gave way to a settled farming culture, scholars agree the nuclear family became the primary unit of social organization, handing down valuable assets such as outbuildings and irrigation ditches. However, a sense of community identity and shared obligations was still needed, at the very least to avoid open conflict between families. On the plus side, sharing agricultural innovations would have been a benefit to the community. An increasing number of archaeologists have reported that megalithic structures required the participation of virtually everyone in the region to build. In effect it was an early form of taxation through sweat equity that produced the first monumental religious and civic centers, defining the center of a larger region. These megalithic centers hosted sacred gatherings for thousands of people at the solstices and equinoxes, reinforcing community identity by celebrating the virtuous qualities of ancestral heroes by singing, dancing, eating, and drinking much more than usual.

Scholars agree that most massive stone structures around the world were built by early farming cultures and were typically designed to represent the setting of creation. Despite the near-universal status of the cosmic egg creation myth, there has been little focus among scholars on the oval form as a core element of ancient megaliths. For example, the egg shape is the primary feature of the oldest megalithic temple in the world at Göbekli Tepe. Before the entire site was buried and abandoned for unknown reasons, it looked like an enormous nest filled with dozens of egg-shaped stone enclosures up to 100 feet across, buttressed internally by stone pillars. Only 15 percent of the site has been excavated due to political conflict in the region. About 5,600 years ago on the island of Malta in the Mediterranean, virtually identical egg-shaped enclosures were built, known as the Mnajdra and Ġgantija temples. Some scholars have suggested the two ovals inside the two temples were meant to appear as a mother goddess figure from above, like the Gravettian Venus, with over-large breasts atop even larger hips.

An egg-shaped enclosure at Göbekli Tepe.

In the village of Carnac on the northwest coast of France in Brittany, the early 20th century Scottish engineer Alexander Thom measured 12 rows of standing stones leading up a hill to a stone mound that he described simply as an "egg." Built about 7,000 years ago, the entire site is located inside an oval outer ring that measures 324 feet on the long axis by 270 feet on the short axis. Nearby is a smaller but nearly identical site of standing stones leading to a stone egg, with the outer oval enclosure measuring 273 feet by 213 feet. Known as the Alignments at Menec, the sites are located at a landfall on a route of the East Atlantic Flyway. British archaeologist Aubrey Burl wrote in *The Stone Circles of Britain, Ireland and Brittany* (2000) that it's inaccurate to use the phrase "stone ring" because "so many are not round but ovoid, egg-shaped." The area around Carnac has the highest concentration of megalithic structures in the world.

Burl catalogued dozens of oval stone rings, with the oldest dating back 5,700 years in Morbihan, just south of Carnac. In Northern Ireland, an oval stone ring in County Sligo could have hosted thousands of people when it was built about 4,750 years ago. The long axis of the oval measured 2,460 feet with a short axis of 1,640 feet. The remains of a 4,500-year-old oval stone ring at Carrowmore in western Ireland measures 1,640 feet by 2,460 feet. Burl believes there were once many more.

At a complex of 23 tombs at Loughcrew in County Meath is a 5,500-year-old oval cairn with a 180-foot circumference that commands the site. Digging at Loughcrew in January 2018, workmen unearthed a six-foot statue of a man with a long, beak-like nose. The unique find was dubbed "The Birdman of Loughcrew," and is currently under the scrutiny of archaeologists.

About 5,200 years ago in the nearby Boinne Valley the ovate megalithic mound known as Brú na Bóinne was built, originally 354 feet on the long axis by 298 feet on the short axis, according to Burl. The fill included thousands of smooth, ovate "river-rolled" quartz stones measuring about six by nine inches.

After an oval ring of standing bluestones was erected at Stonehenge, percussive drumming would have created a resonating acoustic effect, which recent studies have shown has a relaxing influence on brainwaves. Less than two miles east of Stonehenge at a bend in the Avon River is Durrington Walls, once a large settlement contained inside an oval henge measuring 1,700 feet by 1,475 feet, built about 4,600 years ago. The long axis of the Durrington Walls settlement was perpendicular to the southeast horizon where the sun rose on the winter solstice. That was no mistake. The village also had its own astronomical observatory known as a Woodhenge, consisting of a football-field-sized oval ring once encircled by wooden posts 26-feet tall. Other ancient oval forms include:

- The earliest tombs cut in the Valley of the Kings were oval-shaped, cut into high cliffs behind waterfalls about 3,600 years ago. In later years tombs were dug at lower levels and beneath the valley floor, including the tomb of Tutankhamen.

- Built by hunter-gatherers across northwest Finland between 5,500 and 4,000 years ago, Giant's Churches were ovate and aligned to the solstices and equinoxes by doorways and the long/short axis. Among the largest ovals is Kastelli Giant's Church, at 197 feet on the long axis and 115 feet on the short axis.
- The oval ring of standing stones known as Almendres Cromlech near Evora, Portugal features 95 almond-shaped stones up to 11 feet tall erected between 7,000 and 8,000 years ago. The ring measures 230 feet on the long axis and 130 feet on the short axis.
- A perfectly smooth solid stone egg at Monte d'Accoddi in Sardinia measures about six feet in length and is estimated to be about 6,000 years old. Similar-sized stone eggs have been found in Algarve, Portugal, and along the coast.
- About 4,000 years ago in northern Japan, the Jomon culture built the oval Stone Circles by the Oyu River in Honshu Province. By the eastern coast near Mori is a Jomon site at Washinoki featuring an oval pit that contains seven graves.
- In Kyoto, the 1,300-year-old Ishibutai Kofun (tomb) is located inside an oval outer bank.
- The Tabata Stone Circles in Tokyo are oval in shape, erected about 5,500 years ago.
- Built in northern Peru about 2,400 years ago, the stone ring around the village of Chankillo was an oval, with several concentric rings making up the settlement. Above the village on a north-south running ridge are the Thirteen Towers of Chankillo, aligned to both solstices.

Royal Genes and Cosmic Eggs

To align themselves with creator gods who emerged from eggs, kings and queens of the ancient world often claimed the same miraculous origin.

In Africa the Pangwe of the Congo, Cameroon, and Gabon, and the Pygmies of coastal Gabon, say their royal ancestors emerged from eggs. In India, the younger wife of the legendary King Sagara gave birth to an egg-like gourd that burst open to produce 60,000 sons. In the form of a swan, Zeus coupled with Leda, the queen of Sparta, who gave birth to eggs. The Buryat of eastern Siberia believe the whooper swan is the mother of their race, and the eagle is the father.

The Shang Dynasty, which emerged 3,600 years ago to produce the first Chinese music and writing, traced its ancestry to a woman who gave birth after eating an egg that a swallow dropped in her lap. The Koguryo of North Korea describe a river goddess shut away in a room until the rays of the sun caused her to conceive and give birth to a large egg, which hatched a boy who became the first Koguryo king. The Mandaya of the southern Philippines believe the mythic Limokon bird laid two eggs that hatched the first man and first woman. In Hokkaido, Japan, the Ainu tell of a swan that comes down from heaven to save a small boy, the only survivor of a terrible war. The boy married the swan-maiden and they repopulated the tribe. The Kwimiuk tribe of the Algonquin family of tribes in the Great Lakes region say they descended from the loon. Innuits along the southern Alaska coast once identified the mythic bird Yel as their ancestral father, who married the daughter of the sun and together created humans.

Considering the longstanding link between royalty and eggs, it's no great surprise that it was a custom of French and English royalty to design an oval room specifically for the purpose of formally greeting guests and visitors. This meeting room, known as a "levee," was apparently the basis of George Washington's suggestion to build the ovate Blue Room in the White House. The Oval Office may have been based on the Blue Room but wasn't used as a president's office until 1909 under President William Howard Taft.

Cosmic Eggs in the Afterlife

Just 45 miles up the coast from Rome in a volcanic region where two bird flyways converge is the ancient Etruscan city of Tarquinia, where the egg was a symbol of regeneration. Developed between the 8th and 3rd centuries BCE, the city was built on two adjoining plateaus where several streams flow down to the snaky River Marta. Tarquinia is known for its massive necropolis, including 6,000 graves and 200 tombs decorated with outstanding examples of Etruscan frescos. Eggs were painted on vases and frescoes and incised on bronze mirrors. Tarquinian tombs contained painted and engraved ostrich eggs, rare and expensive items made by skilled artisans in the Mediterranean and Near East. Ostrich eggs were placed in tombs in prehistoric Egypt, long before the first pharaoh. In Naqada, an ostrich egg was found in place of the skull on a skeleton. The oldest decorated ostrich egg dates back 60,000 years to Diepkloof Cave in South Africa, where an early human etched a pattern of lines on an eggshell.

The ibis-headed god Thoth.

Beginning about 2,700 years ago Egyptians began mummifying and burying nearly three million egg-shaped jars containing falcons and ibis in tombs up and down the Nile. The complex process of making the jars and mummifying the birds caused an entire industry to be established.

More than 1.75 million mummified falcons and ibis were buried just south of Cairo at Saqqara, with another million entombed at Tuna El-Gebel in Middle Egypt. Real ibis' eggs were scattered among the egg-shaped jars containing the bird remains. A wooden statue of an ibis almost two feet from beak to tail is believed to have originated at Tuna el-Gebel and contains a hidden section inside the rear of the bird. X-rays revealed an oval cavity in the wooden body with the remains of a mummified ibis inside. The statue reflects the Egyptian belief that death was a temporary state not unlike incubation. In ancient Egypt the sarcophagus was referred to as an "egg" in which the soul rejuvenates before being reborn. A similar discovery was made at Dakhla Oasis, where egg-shaped stones were found to contain hidden compartments containing the remains of ibis and raptors.

In ancient Egypt the falcon represented Horus, who traveled between the material world of earth and the upper world of the sun god. The ibis represented the god Thoth, who embodied wisdom, writing, and speech. It was the voice of Thoth that hatched the cosmic egg.

Herodotus related a story he was told in Egypt of the Phoenix making a large egg-shaped ball of myrrh, scooping out the inside, placing the remains of its father inside, and flying it from Arabia to Heliopolis in Egypt for burial at the temple of the Sun. Herodotus noted that the story "does not appear credible."

From Naked Ape to Birdbrain

In *The Naked Ape*, published in 1967, Desmond Morris argued that mankind had inherited the violent, carnivorous aggression of primates, and other writers elaborated on the idea. The radical left protested the book, saying it was an apology for war and the military-industrial complex. The concept was taken to cinematic heights in 1968 by Stanley Kubrick's skull-smashing ape in the opening segment of *2001: A Space Odyssey*.

Now it appears we owe more to birds than apes. A 2014 study showed that humans and birds share about 50 identical genes that are activated when birds learn to sing, and when humans learn to talk. It's long been known that birds and humans both share an unusually high ratio of brain to body size (unlike primates). More recent studies show that bird and human brains also use the same neurological pathways to process information. Both birds and humans interpret and respond to complex social cues as a method of maintaining large, collaborative social groups. In both birds and humans, 75 percent of the brain is made up of frontal cortex, which is dedicated to language, information processing, and social cues.

It's no wonder so many ancient and indigenous cultures identified birds as their ancestral parents. As the coming chapters will show humanity has long expressed a profound identification with birds, from birth to courtship, farming, national identity, war, death, and reincarnation. The cross-cultural myth of avian ancestry suggests an intuitive understanding that humans and birds share many of the same inherent qualities.

Chapter 5

Flight of the Soul

The miraculous cycle of self-regeneration was once perceived as a divine quality of the sun, volcanos, and certain sacred bird species. To have the capacity for self-regeneration was to be immortal.

After a colorful death in the blaze of sunset, the sun is somehow rejuvenated overnight and miraculously reborn in the glow of dawn. The daily miracle of the sun was part of an equally miraculous annual cycle. Every winter the sun falls lower in the sky, its power weakening until the winter solstice when it suddenly begins to rise higher again, growing in strength. The winter solstice was the equivalent of New Year's Day across ancient cultures and was celebrated for a full week.

For ancient cultures that saw the sky as a mirror of the earth, the volcano was the earthly equivalent of the sun, regenerating the earth in a fiery crucible of lava. Half-a-dozen creation stories from Africa, Southeast Asia, Siberia, and North America, describe a source of heat suddenly appearing in the middle of a world-covering primordial ocean, resulting in the production of clouds and the appearance of land.

In China, the sun was once described rising every morning from a presumably volcanic island in the great sea to the east. Another Chinese myth tells of an archer shooting down nine suns, presumably to become volcanos, and leaving the tenth in place. A myth from the Zuni of Arizona includes a volcano identified as "the son of the sun" playing a game of chance. It is perhaps no accident that Zunis associated gambling with volcanos, which could erupt at any time. Prehistoric cultures may not have known that volcanos recharge the soil with an array of precious minerals while layers of ash retain water during droughts, but it didn't require science to observe that volcanic areas tended to be more fertile than others. The spewing out of deadly red and orange lava only set the stage for a vibrant and transformed landscape of blooming vegetation. Some cultures settled in volcanic areas not long after eruptions had occurred.

The Passionate Volcano

Although volcanic eruptions have wiped out human settlements throughout history, volcano mythology doesn't focus on terror and destruction, but on creation, and the passionate feelings of volcano gods.

The eruption of Mt. Mazama in Oregon 7,700 years ago was the largest in the Cascade Range in a million years, and among the largest on Earth in the last 12,000 years. Not long after the volcanic event created Crater Lake, the Modoc and Klamath tribes moved into the area. A Modoc creation story describes the Chief of the Sky Spirits descending to a volcano where he built a lodge and created rivers, animals, fish, and birds. The smoke from the chief's hearth rose through a hole in the roof, but when he dropped a large log on the fire, sparks flew up through the hole and the ground trembled. The chief put out the fire and returned to the sky.

Today, thousands of people live on the flanks of Mount Merapi (Fire Mountain), Indonesia's most active volcano, about 17 miles north of Yogyakarta. On October 25, 2010, and in the weeks following, pyroclastic flows from a major eruption killed 353 people and caused 350,000 residents of the area to flee their homes. Yet the Javanese have long believed the rulers of the spirit kingdom live inside Mount Merapi in a paradise where virtuous ancestors spend the afterlife, complete with roads, vehicles, and domesticated animals.

A mythic story equating volcanos with the passion of human hearts comes from the Koryak of Siberia, who say a Great Raven created men to love women passionately so the tribe would continue. The men were buried in a sacred place where their passionate hearts, burning with love, grew into a volcano. Other myths involve passionate volcano gods caught in love triangles and driven by passion, totally oblivious to humans who might live in the area. In Mesoamerica, the Aztecs believed that Popocatepetl (the Smoking Mountain) and Iztaccihuatl (the White Lady) were lovers who could not bear to be out of each other's sight, and occasionally sent fiery missiles in each other's direction. **Hawaiian** chants tell the story of an explosive and vengeful love triangle among local volcanos. A human heart again plays a role in perhaps the spookiest volcano legend ever told: When the Toltec of Mexico were in decline, and erupting volcanos were visible from the capital city of Tollan, the people gathered for a human sacrifice. The crowd was used to observing human sacrifices, even ritually cutting themselves at the same time to give energy to the gods, but this time they recoiled in a state of true shock and horror when the priest cut open the sacrificial victim's chest only to find he had no heart. This was the end of the Toltec.

The Divinity of Birds

Because migratory birds follow the sun every year as it moves north and south, and because birds can fly so high toward the glowing orb, a universal belief developed that birds were agents and messengers of the sun, and were infused with its divine qualities of self-regeneration.

A fiery example was displayed by the mythical Phoenix, one of many brightly colored firebirds imagined across ancient and indigenous cultures. In its old age, the Phoenix built a nest of spices and sang a song as the rays of the sun set its feathers alight and burned the bird to ashes, from which a new Phoenix emerged. Many scholars believe the Phoenix was a representation of the miraculous daily cycle of the sun. The people of ancient cultures believed the Phoenix was rare, but a real bird. The

Roman naturalist Pliny wrote that a Phoenix was displayed in the Roman senate under Emperor Claudius. The Greek historian Herodotus briefly wrote of the Phoenix, noting he had "never seen one myself."

Hummingbirds were sacred across the Americas partly because of an observable phenomenon in which the bird appears to die soon after sunset only to be reborn at dawn. On cold nights at high altitudes, the hummingbird's metabolic rate drops so low it appears deceased. When the morning sun warms their tiny bodies, they stir back to life. Large waterfowl such as swans, geese, and cranes were sacred across Eurasia and North America partly because the summer molting process of losing and then regrowing their feathers displayed the quality of self-regeneration. As for sacred vultures, naturalists of the ancient world believed they were an all-female species that lived up to 100 years. A 4th century Christian monk wrote that vultures conceived by "turning their womb to the north wind." Fantastic legends about the miraculous birth of various bird species circulated during the Middle Ages, a time when geese were believed to be born from barnacles on driftwood.

Every morning birds find a high perch to catch the first rays of the sun, calling out in a chorus to wake up the rest of the world. In Japan, roosters roamed freely in Shinto temples because their red, saw-shaped combs were symbolic of the rising sun, and because they announced the dawn. The rooster was also the bird of Apollo, the Greek and Roman sun god. Other mythic sun-birds appear in legends from Egypt to China and Peru.

- In ancient China, a crow assisted the sun each day as it rose to the top of the world tree.
- In ancient Heliopolis, city of the sun, the mythical Bennu-bird perched in the Egyptian tree of life, with the sun rising behind it.
- In the American Southwest and Mesoamerica, the bright

primary rainbow colors of the macaw cemented its sacred status as a bird of the sun. Macaws were traded from southern Mexico almost 2,000 miles to Chaco Canyon in New Mexico, where they were kept partly to pluck their feathers for ceremonial use.

- In Peru, Andean art dating back 4,500 years shows the high-flying Andean condor and its 10-foot wingspan as a messenger of the sun god.
- Just 500 years ago, the Incas celebrated Andean condors as divine agents of the sun at the Temple of the Condor at Machu Picchu, located by a serpentine river where two bird flyways converge.

A curious Irish legend tells of mariners coming across an island where a gigantic bird washed itself in a mythical lake. At first the huge bird appeared old and slow-moving but grew younger as it washed itself and soon flew off with great vigor. After a brief discussion, one of the mariners jumped in the lake, splashed around, and never suffered an illness again. The divine quality of self-regeneration was seen as a healing power, and numerous sacred birds were thought to cure the sick, sometimes with the direct aid of the sun. In ancient Greece, the mythic Caladrius bird stared into the eyes of the sick and carried their illness to the sky where the sun burned it away. Like the Phoenix, some believed the Caladrius was a real bird. In ancient Persia, the Zoroastrians described a mythic eagle that healed every illness. Another Persian myth tells of the vulture Saena raising a human boy named Zal, and later healing the wounds of Zal's son Rustam. In Hinduism, the shining Garuda bird healed the sons of Dasharatha after they were badly wounded in battle; "when Garuda touched their faces they were healed."

In the Arabic world, the hoopoe was associated with both spiritual and physical health and is still known as the "doctor bird." In Southeast Asia, the Mentaweian shamans of Indonesia seek cures for illnesses by ascending to the sky in a boat drawn by eagles. In Sumerian, Akkadian, and Babylonian cultures, the healing goddess Gula traveled through the heavens seated on four geese. Native American eagle-bone whistles and flutes were sacred objects used to call eagles to attend curing ceremonies. In folk medicine, the flesh of various bird species was thought to cure everything from snakebites to the common cold. Pliny wrote that rooster meat could cure dysentery, while stork flesh and bird blood was used to treat leprosy. In Hokkaido, Japan, the Ainu press falcon claws on snakebites, and in northern California the Wiyot consider condor feathers to be curative. The Chinese still consider swift soup to be healing, while some Americans still turn to chicken soup in flu season.

The healing power of birds went beyond physical ailments. Lady Rhiannon, of Welsh myth, brought her musical birds to soothe the waking nightmares of battle-scarred warriors. In Ireland, Cliodna of the Fair Hair had three birds that healed the sick with their songs. In numerous Irish legends, the otherworldly music of swans sent listeners to a peaceful slumber, sometimes for days, from which they awoke refreshed. In dramatic performances of sacred healing, the Yakut shaman of Siberia took the form of a loon when traveling to the spirit world to find the lost soul of a patient, which was also in the form of a bird. To retrieve the lost soul, the shaman called out, "my little lark, flutter, fly up! My little bird, chirp and twitter!" The Altaic shaman gathered spirits by beating his drum, mounting a wooden goose, climbing the notches of a birch tree, and singing, "Under the white sky, over the white cloud … rise up to the sky bird!" The shaman would make the call of a goose as he ascended.

The mythic ability of birds to heal and rejuvenate the soul extended beyond the mortal world. In dozens of cultures over thousands of years, the soul either turned into a bird at death or was carried by a bird to the heavens. Infused with the regenerative power of the sun and sent to earth as a benefit to humanity, birds were entrusted with delivering the seeds of vegetation and the care of human souls.

The Sacred Vulture: Queen of the Dead

The oldest and most widespread method of birds conveying human souls to the afterlife is the sky burial, still practiced today by Tibetan Buddhists. The ritual practice consists of leaving bodies to be devoured by vultures, which are believed to fly the soul to a heavenly afterlife.

Numerous cultures saw the vulture as a medicine man, restoring harmony by purifying and cleansing the death scene. Another plausible reason for the mythic status of vultures was their ability to reduce a carcass to a skeleton in just five hours, according to a study at the Texas State University "Body Farm." Hundreds of vultures could reduce a bloody battlefield to bones overnight.

Early practitioners of sky burials paid special attention to the head, once widely believed to be the seat of the soul. The oldest image of a sky burial appears in a 9,000 year-old mural at Çatalhöyük in eastern Turkey, showing two vultures focused on a human head placed on top of a pillar. A variation on the theme was found carved in stone at nearby Göbekli Tepe showing a headless man holding onto a bird that appears to be a vulture. In 2014, an archaeological team concluded that Göbekli Tepe was used only for symbolic or religious purposes. The team also found that villagers in the area had taken the heads of relatives from their graves only to return them sometime later. Perhaps people brought the heads of the year's dead to Göbekli Tepe so vultures would peck through the eye sockets, eat the brain/soul, and carry it away to the heavens. After the ritual, the pecked-clean skulls could be returned to their graves. Seven thousand years later and 7,700 miles away in southern Peru, the Nazca people adopted the sky burial. Nazca artwork depicted condor-like birds eating human parts or holding a trophy head. Simultaneous with the Nazca, the art of the Moche people in northern Peru showed birds pecking at heads or body parts.

Other Soul Guides of the Ancient World

Throughout history and across cultures more than a dozen bird species were thought to convey human souls to the afterlife. From Iceland to Greece and Siberia, souls took on the form of swans or were carried to the heavens by a swan. At funerals for a shaman, the Yakut and Dogan of Siberia placed swan effigies atop a series of poles in ascending height to represent the flight of the shaman's soul. In Norse legend, Valkyries were swan-women who carried dead warriors to Odin at Valhalla. A 6,000-year-old grave in Denmark held an infant covered with the wings of a swan. In Ireland, swans were seen as spirits of the dead. The Greek writer Pausanias described swans singing the soul of a king to the heavens. When Poseidon's son Cycnus was killed in the Trojan War, he turned into a swan.

Between 5,000 and 3,100 years ago on the island of Crete, the Minoan civilization decorated sarcophagi with birds and chariots. Early 20th century archaeologist Bernhard Schweitzer believed the Minoan birds represented an "image of the soul released from the body." Between 3,600 and 3,100 years ago, the Mycenaeans of Greece, birds were the dominant image on pottery buried with the dead. Painted on a wooden Mycenaean ash-chest was a huge, over-sized bird accompanying two warriors to an unknown destination. After the decline of Mycenaean culture birds remained a common image on grave pottery in Greece until about 2,800 years ago. Much later in the Roman classic *Metamorphoses,* Ovid described the ashes rising from King Memnon's funeral pyre taking the form of a bird, "which flew on whirring wings, joined in noisy flight by countless sisters born from the same source."

In ancient Egypt, the goddess Isis and her sister Nephthys took the form of raptors to fly to their murdered brother Osiris, finding him dismembered. Isis miraculously "originated coolness with her wings and wind with her feathers" and brought Osiris back to life. The wings of Isis and Nephthys were carved on the head end of the sarcophagus in the Tomb of Horemheb about 3,500 years ago in the Valley of the Kings. The winged Nephthys also hovers over a large mural depicting the afterlife in the 3,300-year-old Tomb of Seti I.

About 2,700 years ago it became popular in Egypt to place small wooden statuettes of a human-headed bird on the chest of the mummified dead. The three-inch figures represented the *ba* aspect of the human soul, which had the power to fly in the company of the sun god. Infused with the sun's rejuvenating during the day, the *ba* flew back to the tomb at night and transferred the solar energy to the mummified corpse.

The Egyptian Book of the Dead contains transformation spells encouraging the soul of the deceased to become a "divine falcon," a heron, or a swallow. The transformation of the soul into a falcon allowed for the god-like power of flight to the heavens where the soul communes in the spiritual fire of the sun god Re. The transformation of the soul into a heron gave it the qualities of a nurturing mother laying and incubating eggs and hatching new life. The swallow's habit of coming out in large numbers to hunt at dusk may be the reason they were associated with stars and the souls of the dead.

More than 200 "spirit jars" dominated by bird imagery were excavated in Shanghai and dated to between 1,700 and 1,900 years ago. Each had a unique design. While there are no texts to explain the jar's function, most scholars believe they were made to contain souls of the dead. Chinese scholar Kominami Ichirō believes the people depicted on the vessels are conducting a funeral service with help from the painted birds, representing the Hun soul.

In North America, Native American tribes built burial mounds and held sacred ceremonies in which birds played a role in conveying souls to heaven. Cremated human remains were found inside the Rock Eagle Effigy Mound in Putnam County, Georgia, where thousands of pieces of quartz were arranged in the shape of a raptor, measuring 120 feet from head to tail. Another bird effigy mound known as Rock Hawk is thirteen miles to the southeast. At the Native American city of Cahokia in southern Illinois, some of the 270 people buried in Mound 72 were wrapped in beaded blankets patterned in the shape of a bird, including a bird-head near the heads of the deceased. The burial of birds and bird artifacts with human remains may have been intended to infuse the soul of the deceased with the power of flight through the afterlife. Native Americans buried a soapstone human-like figurine with wings and a human head in the Chauga Mound in Oconee County, South Carolina. Once 12-feet high, the mound contained the remains of 30 people. The site showed signs of human habitation dating back 8,000 years.

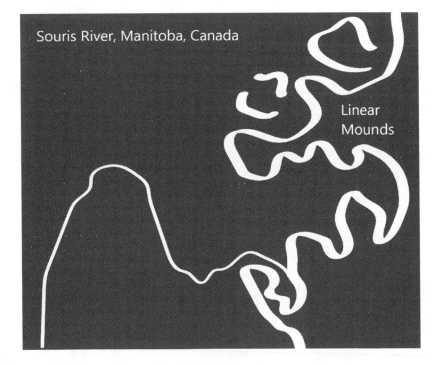

Souris River, Manitoba, Canada

Linear Mounds

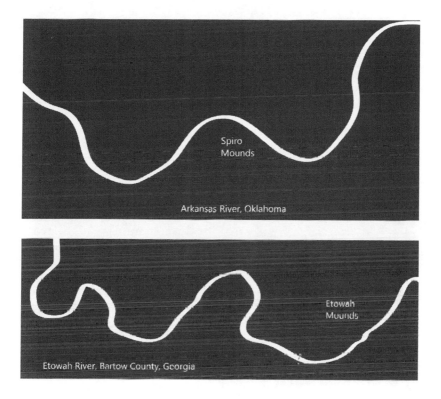

At Spiro Mound in eastern Oklahoma, one of the most common artifacts found with human burials was a small but detailed "Birdman" made from copper. Ceremonial conches and spiral-shaped snail shells decorated to represent the mythic Thunderbird were found buried in the Linear Mounds next to the serpentine Souris River in Alberta, Canada. In Georgia, the Etowah Indian Mounds contained copper plates showing bird men "falcon dancers." The flight of souls was a concept shared across continents and cultures.

Europe

- The Celts of Spain (Celtiberians) believed the souls of the dead on the battlefield went to heaven if eaten by vultures, according to an epic Roman poem by Silius Italicus.

- Scavenging white-tailed eagles were associated with battlefields in Norse and Anglo-Saxon legends.
- The depiction of a dove emerging from the mouth of dying saints appeared in Medieval illustrations, symbolizing the departure of the soul.
- In ancient Germany, a rooster was sacrificed at funerals so its soul would help the human soul to the afterlife.
- In ancient Estonia, a child was found buried with a bird-bone whistle, two bird figurines and crane wings in its hands.
- In Sweden, ravens croaking in a swamp at night were thought to be the victims of murder who were denied a Christian burial.
- For mariners, the gull and albatross were thought to be the souls of lost sailors.
- The Irish considered puffins to be reincarnated monks, while jays were thought to be the souls of druids gathering acorns of the sacred oak. In County Kerry, rooks were the ghosts of cruel landlords who steal vegetables from the peasant's gardens, "Always robbin' from the poor!"

The Mediterranean, Near East, Africa

- Images of the healing hoopoe bird have been found in tombs in Crete and Egypt.
- Peacocks were found carved in tombs and on funerary lamps in Rome.
- A common saying at Turkish funerals is, "His soul bird has flown away."
- The ancient Greek saying for "Drop dead!" was "Go to the crows!"
- In Syria, eagles carved on tombs represented soul-guides.
- In Islamic tradition, the souls of the dead take the form of birds until Judgment Day.

- The soul guide in Jewish tradition is a dove.
- To communicate with dead ancestors, the Senufo of West Africa wore a bird-man mask and wings with genealogical information inscribed on them.

The Americas

- From Canada to Mexico, the whip-poor-will not only foretold death but could locate and capture wandering souls. In nature, the whip-poor-will hunts at night, flying at high speed with its mouth wide open.
- After the death of a Seneca woman a noose was made from the deceased's hair and used to capture a fledgling bird, which was kept in a cage until it began to sing. The bird was then set free to deliver a message of love to the departed in the spirit world.
- Mississippian cultures placed tribal chiefs on a death-bed in the shape of a falcon.
- A wooden bird looking straight up to the sky with wings outspread was attached to the top of a wood casket buried by the Haida on Queen Charlotte Island, Canada.
- The Ghost Dance of Arizona's Cohonino tribe includes climbing a tall pole, kissing the tail feathers of the eagle, flying to the spirit world, and speaking with the dead
- Apache folklore describes a man returning after death as a hummingbird to visit his wife in a meadow.
- In Costa Rica macaws were placed in Bribri burials up to the 17th century.
- Dating back a thousand years, a vulture sculpted from copal resin was buried with gold objects in a tomb at Sitio Conte, Panama.
- In pre-Columbian Tlascala, just east of Mexico City, the elite classes were believed to reincarnate into singing birds.

- Aztec warriors and women who died in childbirth were thought to become hummingbirds in a heavenly garden.
- The remains of vultures and macaws were found in graves throughout the Mayan Empire.
- In Venezuela and Trinidad, the call of cave-dwelling guacharos was thought to be the wailing of ghosts unable to ascend to the heavens due to the weight of their sins.
- Naymlap the first chief of the Sican people on the north coast of Peru, ordered his inner circle to tell his people that he flew away as a bird at death, and to bury him secretly.
- Along the central coast of Peru, macaw feathers were braided into human hair for burials, and mummified parrots were commonly buried.
- In southern Peru, vultures were buried in the tombs of the elite at a Moche site in Pacatnamu. Moche pots show vultures leading a dead human figure to the underworld.

Asia

- As late as the 18th century, the Ostiks of Siberia held funerals where dancers wore bird costumes made of crane skin. Before dying a Yakut chief said he would return as an eagle so his feathers could be used in dances. The Voguls carved bird images on coffins.
- The white heron dance has been performed annually for a thousand years at the Senso-ji Temple in Japan, to purify spirits as they pass from the world.
- In Chinese funeral processions, a paper crane was placed on a chair next to an image of the deceased. Cranes were known to carry immortal heroes to heaven.
- Another Chinese funeral practice calls for a rooster to be placed in a basket on the coffin, crowing on the way to the burial ground.

- Buddhist priests in Guangzhou (Canton) once left rice at the door of temples, believing the birds gathered outside were vessels for ancestral souls.

Australasia

- In New Guinea, the roadrunner's track is made around the deceased. The cassowary embodies the return of female ancestors.
- In New Zealand, the Maori believe seagulls are vessels of ancestral souls and the leaders of the flock are tribal elders.
- In the Kimberley region of northwest Australia, the willie wagtail communicates with spirits of the recently dead, reporting whether the living are speaking ill of them.

People in cultures from around the world have long believed that birds were their soul's ticket to the heavens. Plato said the soul would grow wings after death. Yet the question remains: Where exactly were they going?

Chapter 6

Milky Way Migration

Before the advent of modern science, no one knew the moon was 238,900 miles away, or that traveling millions of light years was required to reach the stars. The celestial bodies, it was commonly believed, were in the general neighborhood of Earth. About 900 years ago, Irish scribes wrote in the *Saltair Na Rann* that the earth was round like an apple (two points for accuracy) and the stars were less than a thousand miles away. Across cultures and continents, people once believed the great rivers of earth were connected to the Milky Way.

- In Irish legend, the Milky Way goddess Boann walked three times around a mythic well that erupted in bright white water to create the Milky Way and the Boyne River in County Meath. One version says the water was so bright that Boann lost sight in one eye.
- In Hinduism, the river goddess Saraswati embodies the flow of water down the Milky Way to the horizon, where it falls on Mt. Meru as snow to melt in the spring, recharging the Ganges.
- In China, the Milky Way was believed to connect with the "heavenly" and "starry" Yellow River in the west, and with deep springs under the vast ocean to the east. The Han River, a tributary of the Yangtze, was also thought to connect with the Milky Way.
- The Barasana of northern Colombia see the Milky Way as a cosmic waterfall on the eastern horizon, sending precious water that flows down the mountains, recharging the Amazon River.
- The modern descendants of the Inca believe that after the

Vilcanota River runs through Cusco, the oldest city in the Americas, it joins up with the Milky Way on the horizon.

- In ancient Egypt the Milky Way goddesses Hathor and Isis were associated with the rising of certain stars in June, coinciding with the Nile's annual flooding.

The Milky Way appears to intersect with a mountain.

The Milky Way is universally described as a river, a path, or a road. Spanning 60 degrees across the southern sky, the ancient Greeks saw the constellation Argo Navis as a sailing ship in the Milky Way, complete with a keel, poop deck, and sails. The Greeks completed the portrait of a riverine ecosystem with constellations that looked like fish, eagles, crows, and water snakes.

It's in the nature of a river to carry things with it, and for cultures around the world the Milky Way carried souls, with various species of waterfowl leading the migratory journey. The constant vocalization of waterfowl in flight was taken as soothing songs to comfort the tattered souls carried by the birds. In the Baltic States, Central Asia, and Siberia, the Milky Way was known as "the path of birds," specifically for migratory waterfowl such as ducks, geese, swans, and cranes. The same cultures also knew the Milky Way as the "route of dead souls." Similarly in North America, the Milky Way was known both as the road of souls and the path of birds. A romantic variant of the Milky Way/migratory bird myth can be found in Estonia, where the Milky Way goddess Lindu, Queen of the Birds, took the form of a white bird with a woman's head. Lindu fell in love with the Northern Lights and the pair were engaged, but the Northern Lights disappeared before their wedding day. Lindu's tears fell on her wedding veil, which became the Milky Way. From that point on, migrating birds followed the trail of stars in her veil. If the Milky Way was just a cosmic migratory flyway, what was the destination? Where was the soul-bearing birds' seasonal ground?

The Heavenly Celestial Pole

Each hemisphere has its own celestial pole. Both are visual illusions created by the spinning Earth, making it appear that all the stars circle around a single point, the hub of the universe. For people seeking patterns in the sky, this one stood out: A great wheel of stars turning around an unmoving island in space.

A time-lapse photo of the northern celestial pole.

When the people of ancient cultures looked to the northern celestial pole, they saw Draco the serpent turning closely around it with Cygnus the swan always hovering above. Gazing at the southern celestial pole, ancient cultures identified Hydrus, the water snake turning closely around it, and nearby Apus, the bird of paradise. Below Apus and Hydrus, Corvus the crow stands on the back of Hydra the larger water snake. The fact that cultures thousands of miles apart identified a mythical bird and snake circling both the northern and southern celestial pole suggests a near-universal belief projected on a random arrangement of stars. The cosmic birds and serpents inhabiting a heavenly paradise at the celestial pole was a match for where they lived, an idyllic earthly landscape where migratory birds fly over serpentine rivers. Of all 88 official constellations the two creatures most well represented are birds (9) and snakes (6).

Perhaps the most literal description of the soul's afterlife journey to the heavenly celestial pole is found in the Finnish epic *Kalevela*, which describes swans flying souls of the dead to a warm place beyond the horizon, and then up the Milky Way, known as *Linnunrata* or Path of the Birds. As the soul-bearing swans approach the northern celestial pole, a swirling wind caused by the turning bowl of the sky pulls them out through a small hole to a heavenly land of rest called *Tuonela*. Ultimately the swans complete their round-trip migration and return the healed and rejuvenated 'new' souls to pregnant mothers on Earth. A similar Ukrainian legend describes birds spending winters in heaven and returning in spring with eggs.

The Finns' notion of soul flight to the celestial pole may stem from their observation of whooper swans migrating southeast in late fall, heading toward a point where the distant horizon met the Milky Way. In the imagination of those who forged the myth, the swans flew beyond the horizon of the material world and into the spirit world of the Milky Way, where Cygnus the swan could be seen flying north towards the celestial pole. The Finns may have observed that the smattering of red neck feathers on the earthly whooper swan seemed to match the orange and red tinges of some of the stars that make up Cygnus. During the cold months of winter, Cygnus appears to fly up and around the pole, as if tending a nest. As spring arrives, Cygnus appears to dive toward earth again. In Norse myth, unborn souls wait in the Fountain of Urd (a stand-in for the celestial pole) to be gathered by storks, which deliver souls to the wombs of expectant mothers. Slavic cultures also believed the stork delivered human infants. In Hawaii, the frigate bird is believed to return babies from heaven. A tradition on the Malay Peninsula in Southeast Asia is for an expectant mother to eat a bird at the base of a sacred tree just before delivering her child, or the soul will not be joined to the infant.

The Divinity of Turning

What exactly made the celestial pole so special? What was the source of its divine rejuvenating power? Perhaps the crucial aspect is that the entire universe appears to turn around the pole, leaving it fixed and unmoving, an island outside the cycles of time and the seasons. The druid Taliesin described the northern celestial pole as "the pin of pivotal space." The Navajo name for the pole and the circumpolar stars turning closely around it is Nahookos, meaning to turn. An axle-like pole was imagined to fit into the celestial hub of the universe like the handle of a twirling cosmic umbrella, wielding the awesome power to stir the cauldron of stars, space, and time. Across cultures the celestial pole has been described as a fountain, the navel of the universe, a whirlpool, a cauldron, a glittering palace, a celestial mill, the sky nail, Vishnu's Toe, and Buddha's Nandana Grove.

In recent millennia, when Polaris was closest to the celestial pole, most Native American tribes called it the "Star That Does Not Move," or the "Not-Walking Star." Yet some also identified Polaris as an immortal deity commanding the sky that turned around it. The Luiseno and Maricopa of southern California called Polaris "Sky Chief" and "Captain" respectively, while the Pomo of Northern California called it "The Eye of the Creator." Originally from Nebraska and Kansas, the Pawnee saw Polaris as the supreme being Tirawa, chief of all stars. Tirawa was the One Above, changeless, and supreme, the one who originally placed all the stars carefully and deliberately in the sky, then sprinkled the heavens with a band of crystal chips to form the Milky Way.

In many ancient cultures, a spinning "fire driller" turned the universe around the celestial pole at creation, lighting a "cosmic fire" at the pole that produced the sun, moon, and stars, according to archaeoastronomer Michael A. Rappenglück of Gilching Observatory in Germany. The celestial bird Cygnus was described stealing the cosmic fire and bringing it to earth, signifying the origins of human culture. This ability to fly between the spirit world of the cosmos and the earthly realm would become the primary mythical and religious role of birds.

In the Hindu legend, The Churning of the Ocean of Milk, weary gods returning from battle used a mythic snake to turn a polar mountain, causing the stars to rotate faster and faster until they bestowed gifts, including a physician, a gem for Vishnu, a flying elephant for Indra, the pipal (fig) tree, the coconut palm tree, and finally Surabhi, a cow with a woman's head that provided a healing elixir of cosmic milk. The mythic snake that spun the celestial pole likely represented the Draco constellation, which is always visible turning closest around the northern celestial pole. In ancient Greece, the Rod of Asclepius depicted a snake turning around a pole, symbolizing healing and medicine. The Greek Bowl of Hygieia showed a snake turning around a bowl or chalice, symbolizing pharmaceutical medicine.

The cosmic turning action is also found in the Japanese creation story, which describes a divine couple standing on a celestial bridge and using long poles to stir the primordial mass of earth, forming the first island of Japan. The couple then descended to the island and built a palace with a large pillar which they circled around to procreate and form the other islands, gods, and creatures. In Navajo astronomy, a celestial father and mother circle around the star Polaris, known as the Central Fire, a celestial match for the fireplace in the family Hogan. The cosmic father is a chief and a warrior while the mother turns a grinding stone and stirring stick to provide nourishment.

In ancient China, a legend described the emperor being infused with divinity when the pole star shined its light on his mother as she gave birth to him. Later in Chinese history, Confucius taught that the economy revolved around the emperor just as circumpolar stars turn around the celestial pole. The physical layout of ancient Chinese cities lined up with various constellations, with the emperor's palace at the center, representing the pole. Similarly in Nebraska, the Skidi Pawnee established villages that aligned with their constellations, each of which carried a spiritual meaning. As the constellations rose and set through the seasons, a ceremony was held in every corresponding village. The annual cycle of rolling rituals began in spring with the "First Thunder" ceremony, held in the village symbolizing Tirawa, the supreme being identified with the celestial pole.

Circumpolar Superstars

The Milky Way was the road of the dead across numerous cultures, but there was also a shorter path to the celestial pole and the stars that turned around it, earned by those who gave their final breath in sacrifice for others.

Those who died for the community were elevated to an immortal status, their souls spending eternity among the circumpolar stars that never set below the horizon, always shining high in the night sky as a beacon and model for future generations. In Norse myth, Valkyries collected the souls of Viking warriors and flew them directly to Valhalla. In China, storks took warriors to the heavens. The Pawnee believed the Milky Way was the Path of Departed Spirits except for warriors killed in battle, who took the "short path."

In ancient Egypt, the pharaohs were rewarded for their sacrifice in service to the people by spending eternity among the never-setting circumpolar stars. In the Pyramid Texts the pharaoh says, "May you lift me and raise me to the Winding Waterway (Milky Way), may you set me among the gods, the Imperishable Stars." In the Pyramid Texts, the preferred destination of the soul was the "White Palace of the great ones at the [end of the] Beaten Path of the Stars," where the soul would live forever on "the Islands of the Righteous."

In the Hindu *Mahābhārata*, those who gave their life for others received eternal rest in the cosmos. "And those brilliant regions that are seen from the earth, there he beheld (those) who had yielded up their lives, stationed in their respective places." The enigmatic Celts were not so literal. The 4th century Welsh poet Taliesin wrote that only worthy souls could eat from the Dagda's cauldron, which was located inside a castle always turning in the northern sky. Taliesin wrote that the cauldron "will not boil the coward's portion."

In China, a meticulously recreated riverine landscape populated by 46 life-sized bronze sculptures of waterfowl was discovered in

Shanxi Province as part of a massive underground tomb complex built for China's first emperor, Qin Shi Huang. Archaeologists believe the river scene represented the heavenly garden where the emperor would enjoy the afterlife. The 20 bronze swans, 20 wild geese, and six cranes were sculpted in a variety of poses. Amidst the birds were 15 terra cotta human figures, who some believe represent musicians. In life, Emperor Huang comported himself as a semi-divine being and sent two expeditions to locate the legendary Fusang Tree on a mythic island in the Pacific Ocean (both failed). Despite Emperor Huang's endless pursuit of an elixir of immortality, he died in 210 BCE.

Across cultures, souls that qualified for a direct ascent were pharaohs and kings, warriors who died on the battlefield, hunters who died in the chase, women who died in childbirth, martyrs and others who gave their lives so others could live. A similar cosmic image was evoked by Senator Robert F. Kennedy during the Democratic Convention of 1964, when he publicly spoke about his slain brother John F. Kennedy for the first time. "When I think of President Kennedy, I think of what Shakespeare said in *Romeo and Juliet:* 'When he shall die, take him and cut him out into stars, and he shall make the face of heaven so fine that all the world will be in love with night, and pay no worship to the garish sun.'"

Bird on a Pole

Ancient texts and sacred art across numerous cultures suggest the bird-on-a-pole symbol reflects the star-bird Cygnus hovering above the northern celestial pole, overseeing the cosmos and the afterlife.

Certainly, a bird perching atop a tree is a common sight in nature, with many species displaying an innate desire to sit on fence posts, telephone poles, roof ridges, church spires, or some other lofty vantage point. In ancient cultures, the symbol of a bird on a pedestal appeared on everything from Phoenician coins to the zodiac at the temple of Denderah in Egypt. In Cameroon, a ceramic bird perches atop a pole that extends from a calabash holding the bones of ancestors. Birds carved from soapstone decorate the tops of pillars at the Great Zimbabwe Ruins, an egg-shaped megalith thought to be constructed about 800 years ago.

A rendering of the death scene at Lascaux Cave.

The oldest known bird-on-a-pole symbol was painted in Lascaux Cave in southern France about 17,000 years ago. The simple outline of a songbird is perched atop a long straight line or pole, right next to a dead man and the dead body of a large bison-like animal. Other details confirm the man was a hunter who clearly died while trying to obtain food for the community. The bird on a pole may have been a sign that the hunter's soul flew directly to the celestial pole, and the process and completion of the painting itself may have been part of a funeral service. It was once a widespread belief that cave walls were a membrane through which spirits could travel from the material to the spirit world. In that case, the journey of the hunter's soul to the afterlife was not the only concern, as indigenous cultures have been known to hold rituals facilitating the reincarnation of animal souls as well, so they would return in animal form to be hunted again.

As Above, So Below

As the seasons turn, the Milky Way slowly goes through a series of twisting movements across the night sky. During mid-summer the Milky Way appears relatively high up as a straight line, but by mid-winter it appears in the shape of an arch, an illusion caused by its lower position in the sky.

Our distant ancestors perceived many things in the stars of the night sky. The changing shape of the Milky Way, what time of year it crossed the horizon, and what landscape features it connected with (mountains, rivers) all contributed to stories reenacted in the seasonal sacred theater of ancient cultures. The circumpolar northern constellation Lyra was originally a vulture in the ancient Near East but was later identified as a harp by the ancient Greeks. It may also be the harp carried by the Irish Dagda, who brought the magic instrument with him from 'fairyland' to Ireland. The Navajo tell Winter Stories from October to February based on the movement of the stars.

In Australia, the Boorong of northwest Victoria named southern constellations after owls, crows, wedge-tailed eagles, and the malleefowl. For Aboriginals the Milky Way is an emu with its head close to the southern celestial pole. Halfway around the world in Peru, the Inca saw the Milky Way as a cosmic baby llama suckling its mother, still attached by the umbilical cord. As constellations rose and set, all manner of creatures appeared on the horizon, following each other across the night sky and taking their parts in the unfolding panorama of spoken legends. When the body of the emu rises above the Australian horizon in April and May it's mating season, but when its legs drop below the horizon in July the emu becomes a "nest-sitter." A celestial toad rises just as earthly toads end their hibernation and start croaking.

More than 4,000 years ago, the name for the Milky Way under the Akkadian Empire was Snake River. The Hindus of northern India referred to the Milky Way as the Path of the Snake while the Norse referred to it as Jörmungandr, or world serpent. The

Navajo depicted the Milky Way with a series of diamond shapes not unlike snakeskin. Parts of the Milky Way could easily be perceived as rivers, including a long snaky segment, islands, and a major tributary overflown by Cygnus. The snake moniker for the Milky Way may also have reflected its annual change in appearance from straight to curved. At some point in time, it seems our distant ancestors began to perceive the Milky Way as a cosmic mirror, guiding them to an eco-paradise on earth. The record shows that human-like species consistently settled where bird flyways converged on long segments of serpentine rivers, often featuring islands and marshes. As above, so below.

Marshy areas are a favorite habitat for waterfowl. In South Africa, the Zulu myth of creation tells of the sky god Umvelingangi descending from heaven to create a mythical marsh known as Uthlanga. The Zulu creator god Unkulunkulu, meaning "ancestor," grew out of a reed in the marsh. In the Yoruba religion of West Africa, the God Obatala descended from heaven to the watery marshes of earth and used sand and a chicken to make soil. In the sacred Egyptian city of Abydos, just north of the largest bend in the Nile River, an inscription dedicated to pharaoh Seti I describes "the marshes of the gods, the place from which the birds come ... beyond the horizon, before the creation..." In the Egyptian afterlife, if the soul was found to be light as a feather it could fly to the paradise known as The Field of Reeds.

Long before the arrival of Europeans, Australian Aboriginals identified Cuddie Springs and the adjacent Macquarie Marsh in New South Wales as the site of a Dreamtime story about Mullyan the giant eagle hawk, which built a nest high in a yaraan tree. Today, BirdLife International has identified Macquarie Marsh as an Important Bird Area, featuring more than 200 bird species, encompassing an area the size of Yosemite National Park.

In addition to marshes, prime bird habitat is found on islands with meandering coastlines, protected coves, and tidal pools, partly because many islands have no significant predators. Some of the world's oldest cities originated on river islands, including the Île de la Cité in Paris and Museum Island in Berlin. Cross-cultural myths and legends describe islands as where life began, where medicinal plants were found, and where souls are uplifted to a harmonious utopia.

Texts from the Egyptian Temple of Edfu tell of an island called the Homeland of the Primeval Ones, a paradise where most of the gods died in a flood. Those who survived came to Egypt as builders and farmers who sowed seeds. In a country featuring hundreds of islands, it's little wonder the ancient Greeks wrote about them often. After death it was believed the soul had to be admitted four times to the island of Elysium, where honey-sweet fruit grows, before being permanently taken to the Islands of the Blessed. There was ongoing speculation in Greek literature that Elysium was an actual island in the Aegean. Historian Diodorus Siculus wrote of an island known as Hyperborea located in the "far north" where a choral service was said to be performed harmoniously with swans, who flew down from the mountains on the spring equinox.

The Celts believed the sea god Manannán journeyed back and forth to the afterlife where he ruled from the island of Emhain Ablach. Irish legends are full of voyages to bizarre islands, including one where a man covered in hair tends to his family of bird-children. Some islands were described as real but magical places. A legendary island known as Hy-Brasil was said to appear every seven years off the western coast of Ireland. In 1872, antiquarian T.J. Westropp wrote that he saw Hy-Brasil appear out of the sea. The debate over the existence of magical islands may originate with the phenomenon of Fata Morgana, which occurs when sunlight is refracted through a temperature inversion, creating a mirage. During Arctic explorations, Fata Morgana tricked numerous mariners into exploring new lands that would only fade away as the inversion lifted.

It wasn't only the presence of serpentine rivers, marshes and islands filled with birds that mirrored the stars. The blazing lava of volcanoes was considered the earthly equivalent of the sun. Year-round freshwater springs were mirrors of the celestial pole. The fiery sunset was a bed of colorful flowers in the clouds. The refraction of light from gems and rock crystals was equated with stars twinkling in the night sky, giving off hints of color. Connecting earth to the spirit world of the cosmos was the world tree. In Russian legend, a miraculous source of food and healing flows from under the alatyr stone at the base of the world tree, guarded by the serpent Garafena and the bird Gagana.

From underneath the little stone,
from underneath the white Latyr,
Rivers flowed, swift rivers,
All over the earth, all over the universe –
To bring healing for the whole world,
To bring food for the whole world ...

Chapter 7

Birds, Serpents & the World Tree

In modern folklore, a boy plants a magic bean and discovers the next morning that a beanstalk has grown so high that it disappears into the clouds. An even more outlandish visual picture was reflected in myths of the world tree, described with its roots in underground springs and its highest branches reaching to the stars.

Symbolically, the world tree was much like the polar mountain. Both were perceived as connecting the earthly realm to the hub of the universe at the celestial pole. Both were symbols of a cosmic water cycle that was also a conduit for souls. The practice of walking around a sacred mountain to activate a spiritual connection with the heavens is also practiced around world trees. Devout Hindus bury urns beneath Bodhi trees and walk around the tree seven times each morning. Buddhists circumambulate the stupa, a structure with a central pole intended to represent the Bodhi tree.

The polar mountain and the world tree also display a physical resemblance that was likely perceived as powerful evidence of a universal truth. The world tree's highest and smallest branches were like the trickle of headwaters high on a mountain, the larger middle branches like creeks converging lower down the mountain, and the tree trunk like the main river that runs into the valley below. At the base of the tree was a snake, embodying serpentine rivers. Perched at the top was a bird.

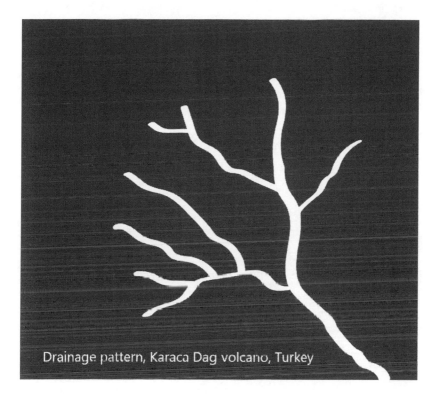

Drainage pattern, Karaca Dag volcano, Turkey

Scholarly references to the world tree typically cite Yggdrasil, the mighty ash of Norse mythology, with an eagle at the top and a dragon at its base, but the true age of the motif is unknowable. A world tree legend appeared in the first Sumerian writing about 5,000 years ago, describing King Etana seeking out a divine tree with a sacred eagle in its branches and a serpent guarding the base. In Central China's Sichuan Province, three bronze "trees of life" more than 10 feet high were excavated in the 1990s and found to be about 3,200 years old. Each tree featured a Phoenix-like bird at the top and a dragon at the base. Scholars believe the trees represent the mythic Fusang, believed to grow on a remote island in the Pacific where the sun rises.

A cross-cultural review suggests that world trees were chosen for a common set of biological traits that reinforce their cosmological meaning. One essential quality was an outstanding ability to attract birds, either with winter-blooming fruits and berries or especially fragrant flowers in spring that attract insects, caterpillars, and moths. More than half of all bird species eat the fruits of flowering trees and distribute their seeds in droppings. Some dig caches to store nuts such as acorns, which often sprout before the bird returns. The tree helps the bird, and the bird helps the tree: It's a classic symbiotic relationship that's existed for millions of years. "The tree is given birth to by the bird," is a phrase found in two Bantu dialects of South Africa, where indigenous tribes still limit hunting the guinea fowl, which eats insects and seeds. Also protected is the thorn acacia tree, a habitat of the guinea fowl.

Today, science is catching up with ancient wisdom once again. In Cambridgeshire, England, a 2021 study by the UK Centre for Ecology and Hydrology found that jays burying acorns played a crucial role in regenerating an oak forest. A study by the University of São Paulo in Brazil found bird species that distribute seeds from the widest variety of trees enjoy what's known as "macroevolutionary stability" over millions of years, as reported in the May 2021 issue of *Science*. Seed-distributing birds also tend to "produce daughter species" more frequently to make up for extinctions. In addition to having an outstanding ability to attract birds, other traits commonly found in a world tree include:

- Runs with milky sap, and/or produces white flowers, fruit, or has white bark, symbolically representing the Milky Way.
- Produces nutritious and healing milky drinks made from fruits or nuts.
- Has medicinal properties in most or all of its parts.
- Grows to great heights.
- Has an unusually long lifespan, including the oldest in the world (the yew).
- Is among the first vegetative species to repopulate and

heal damaged landscapes.

- Produces oval-shaped leaves, fruits, or nuts.
- Demonstrates seemingly miraculous regenerative and transformational qualities.

After cutting a hazel or an oak down to the stump, a common ancient practice known as coppicing, the trees regenerate themselves in a different form. Rather than growing back normal thick branches, they produce long and flexible rods. This natural response to injury was widely perceived as a miracle of regenerative and transformative healing. Like priapism, it may also have been perceived as another literal example of sympathetic magic, revealing the metaphysical pole that connected earth and sky. The Greek messenger god Hermes, carried a hazel rod or wand entwined with snakes and topped by a pair of wings (symbolic of the World Tree) to conduct the souls of the dead to the underworld. Irish kings were depicted holding hazel rods, signifying royal lineage. The etymology of the modern word "wand" traces back to Old Norse and Proto-Germanic, meaning flexible rod or switch. Modern folklorists trace the magic wand back to the rod of Aaron in the Hebrew Bible, which sprouted an almond tree overnight as a demonstration of the Hebrew god Elohim's power.

In Iranian mythology, divine birds took sprigs from a shining white Haoma tree growing in a mountain paradise and flew them down to earth to be cultivated by humans. Although the Haoma may or may not have been based on a real tree, Zoroastrians were said to make a ritual drink from it that bestowed health, fertility, and immortality. Coppicing the Haoma tree was said to produce offshoots known as Barsom, which were used in Zoroastrian rituals. Scholars have noted that the legend and traits of the Haoma tree are identical to the Hindu plant and ritual drink known as Soma. The following are summaries of the biological traits of 12 world trees and their symbolic meaning across cultures. An additional 14 can be found in the appendix.

Hazel

Biology/Ecology: Growing only up to 20 feet in height, the hazel is a bushy tree with ovate leaves that blooms in late winter, producing nuts with a nutritious milky center that were a significant part of the Neolithic diet in western Europe. Hazel rods were also commonly used to build shelters at the time, suggesting the practice of coppicing dates back at least 10,000 years. Hazel wood was more recently used to make tool handles and walking sticks.

Religious/Medicinal: In Irish legend, nine hazelnut trees grew in a heavenly paradise where they dropped their nuts into a sacred well that erupted in a spray of blazing white water and spilled over to form the Boyne River. The hazelnuts were said to cause bubbles of inspiration in the river, much to the benefit of thirsty artists. An Irish folktale says that every seven years, drinking water from the River Boyne bestows the gift of spontaneous poetry. A Scottish legend describes a man named Farquhar cutting hazel branches from a bush when six brown snakes emerged from its base and wriggled away. Farquhar kept his wits enough to catch a seventh snake, which was pure white. While boiling the snake, steam emerged from the pot and infused Farquhar with the knowledge of all medicine. In a German folk tale, the snake that lived beneath a hazel tree had magical wisdom. The fictional Cinderella plants a hazel branch at her mother's grave that grows into a tree where her wishes are granted by birds.

Oak

Biology/Ecology: The mighty oak tree grows up to 150 feet in height and lives more than 1,000 years. In ancient Greece, the word for oak also meant tree. When coppiced, the oak sprouts rod-like branches. A wide variety of birds routinely nest in its many natural cavities while caterpillars and butterflies attract migrating warblers, tanagers grosbeaks, woodpeckers, and orioles. In fall, acorns are a bumper crop for crows and blue jays.

Religious/medicinal: In Ireland a magical harp made of oak was said to be carried from the spirit world by the semi-divine chief Dagda. In County Kildare, a 450-foot magical oak was said to appear in the village of Mugna at the birth of a legendary king, producing three crops a year of acorns, nuts, and apples (County Kildare was originally Cill Dara, meaning Church of the Oak). Archaeologists found an oak post at the center of a large circle at the site of Emain Macha, known as the castle of the Red Knights near the modern town of Armagh. Druids often taught their students under large white oaks.

Sycamore Fig

Biology/Ecology: The sycamore runs with white (latex) sap, grows up to 65 feet tall along the Nile and can live up to 600 years. Filled with white fruit and a red center, the figs were once made into a milky paste that was fed to newborns. Like hazel and oak trees, the sycamore responds to coppicing by producing thin, flexible rods.

Religious/Medicinal: In the ancient Egyptian tomb of King Thutmose III, the sycamore tree of Mother Hathor (also the Milky Way goddess) was shown with breasts, from which the king drank the milk of rebirth. The aspect of soul known as the *Ba* was depicted as a bird with a human head drinking from the sycamore tree, which was commonly planted around tombs. The sycamore fig's fruit, sap, and bark were used for more than a dozen ailments. The wood was used to make coffins.

Yew

Biology/Ecology: Yew trees and bushes can live more than 3,000 years by continually regenerating themselves. As the main trunk dies, new shoots rise from the base to become a new tree. Sometimes a drooping branch burrows below ground, develops a root system, and becomes a separate tree. Smaller yew bushes respond well to trimming and are often shaped into topiary. The yew has a symbiotic relationship with cedar waxwings and thrushes, which gorge on its red berries all winter. Birds make yew seeds viable by breaking down their tough coating before dispersing them.

Religious/Medicinal: An Irish legend tells of an enchanted yew on an island in Loch an Iuir (Lake of the Yew) in Donegal that was linked to a heavenly paradise, according to *Irish Trees*, by Niall Mac Coitir. This link to paradise sheds light on the Celtic Chieftain 'Catuvolcus' choice to eat poisonous yew berries as a form of suicide rather than surrender to the Romans as a slave. In Celtic Brittany, the roots of a yew growing in a cemetery were said to extend into the mouths of the dead, presumably as a vehicle for souls to rise to heaven. Druids planted yews at sacred wells, temples, and burial sites. Some Celtic tribes were named after yews, signifying the tree's connection to the world of ancestral spirits. A remote grove of yews was considered a place of healing for men driven mad by warfare, such as "Mad Sweeney," who fled to a valley of yews at Glenn Bolcain. William Wordsworth found the yew tree snake-like: "...each particular trunk a growth of intertwisted fibres serpentine up-coiling..."

Baobab

Biology/Ecology: Native to Africa, Madagascar and Australia, the baobab grows up to 100 feet and can live more than 2,000 years. A baobab in Zimbabwe was documented to be 2,450 years old when it died in 2011, making it the oldest flowering plant ever recorded. The baobab's white, yellow or red flowers open briefly around dusk and fade by the next morning. The large oval fruits contain dry white pulp used for medicinal purposes.

Religious/Medicinal: The people of Madagascar routinely leave gifts at the base of a baobab because they believe the spirits of dead family members live in the trunk. The baobab's leaves, bark, and seeds have been used to treat malaria, tuberculosis, and toothache, while the white pulp is used to reduce fever and stimulate the immune system.

Coconut Palm

Biology/Ecology: Found across India and Southeast Asia, the coconut palm rises to a height of about 80 feet, producing 50 to 100 ovoid coconuts annually. The white fruit, with a high fat content, is grated and mixed with water to make coconut milk. Some palms self regenerate by producing new shoots from the base that become new trees.

Religious/Medicinal: In Hindu legend, the coconut palm grew in Lord Indra's garden on the mythical Mt. Meru at the center of the world, a place of rebirth and reincarnation. The tree was one of many healing gifts from the mythic Churning of the Ocean of Milk, when the gods used a serpent to spin a polar mountain, thus speeding up the turning of stars around it. For more than 2,000 years, coconut milk has been used in Hindu temples for the sacred baths of deities.

Sacred Fig

Biology/Ecology: Growing up to 100 feet, the sacred fig (*Ficus religiosa*) is a semi-evergreen native to India that runs with white sap and is also known as the Bodhi tree. The flowers bloom in February with large red petals surrounding a white cup-like feature topped with purple and yellow tendrils.

Religious/Medicinal: Known to grow wild in the foothills of the

Himalayas, Hindu texts say Lord Indra planted a sacred fig on the polar Mt. Meru, at the center of heaven. The Buddha was said to attain enlightenment after meditating for six days under a Bodhi tree. All parts of the tree, including its white sap, have been used in traditional medicine to cure about 50 different ailments.

Silver birch

Biology/Ecology: In Europe the silver birch grows up to 50 feet with white papery peeling bark and slender drooping branches.

Religious/Medicinal: In Siberia, the silver birch was the world tree of the Yakut, who believed the first man at creation was fed from breasts half-emerging from its white trunk. Also in Siberia, the Goldi, Dolgan, and Tungus people describe souls waiting to be born as birds perched in birch tree branches. When the Siberian shaman performed a spirit journey to find souls and meet the supreme being atop the world tree, he climbed a birch while pretending to ride on the effigy of a white goose. In Celtic areas of Germany and Scotland, bodies were buried with hats made of birch, which was thought to grow at the gates of paradise. An Irish burial custom calls for wrapping the body in bushy birch branches before burial.

Yaraan

Biology/Ecology: Growing only along the rivers of Australia, the yaraan is a red gum tree with a white trunk and white flowers that bloom in groups of seven or nine.

Religious/Medicinal: The Aboriginals of New South Wales in southeastern Australia say the Milky Way was a huge yaraan tree that grew up from the earth at Creation, with white cockatoos roosting in its branches. The yaraan showed its sadness at the death of people by weeping red tears on its white trunk and enabled the soul of the first man to reach his cosmic afterlife.

Eastern white pine

Biology/Ecology: Native to the Northeastern United States and Canada, eastern white pines have been documented to grow up to 230 feet and live up to 500 years.

Religious/Medicinal: In the 16th century, the chiefs of the Five Nations Confederacy met under an Eastern white pine to negotiate a peace agreement, and the tree became the centerpiece of the confederacy's official seal. The Chippewa used the white pine's antimicrobial pine resin in a poultice with a wet pulp of white inner bark to treat wounds and infections. Native Americans commonly dried and pounded the pine's soft white inner bark to produce flour.

Ceiba

Biology/Ecology: With a base more than 65 feet across and growing more than 200 feet, the ceiba tree has been known to live more than 400 years. Native from Mexico to South America, its white, cotton-like seedpods, known as kapok, float easily in the air. Ceiba flowers are creamy-white and pink toward the edges, and its nectar routinely attracts the sacred hummingbird.

Religious/Medicinal: The Mayan creator Xibalba was said to raise the ceiba tree at creation. The massive tree has large conical thorns on its trunk, which are reproduced on Maya funerary urns. The Maya created a shrine to the ceiba in Balamkanche Cave in the Yucatan, where they found a natural column formed by a stalagmite joined with a stalactite. The ceiba is the national emblem of Puerto Rico and Guatemala, with some of the oldest specimens towering over public gathering places in the cities of Puerto Rico, Guatemala, and Honduras. Some Amazonian tribes of eastern Peru say that deities live in the ceiba's branches.

Tobacco

Biology/Ecology: Flowering tobacco produces star-shaped blooms from white to pink and yellow, attracting hummingbirds and butterflies. It's plausible that various creatures closely associated with tobacco were part of its cosmological importance. Feeding on tobacco leaves, the tobacco hornworm molts five times during the larval period, finally burrowing into the ground and emerging as a tobacco hawk moth with wavy white lines and equally spaced white dots on the edges of its wings. It was likely meaningful to Native Americans that the tobacco flower and the tobacco hawk moth both featured white, star-like features.

Religious/Medicinal: Often carried in medicine bundles, tobacco was considered a gift of healing medicine from the creator across virtually every Native American culture. In the Caribbean, an Arawak legend tells of a hummingbird flying on the back of a crane and bringing tobacco seeds from the heavens. A Cherokee legend describes a hummingbird stealing tobacco from geese. Archaeologists believe the Adena culture of southern Ohio began growing tobacco about 3,000 years ago, with more intense cultivation starting a thousand years later in the same area by the Hopewell culture. Both cultures made sacred tobacco pipes in the shape of birdmen. In the Southwest, the remains of cultivated tobacco found in High Rolls Cave in New Mexico were estimated to be 3,400 years old. Tobacco is an ancestral clan symbol of the Hopi, Zuni, Navajo, Mohave, and Pueblo tribes. It was commonly used in rituals and its smoke was believed to carry prayers to the heavens.

The Baníwa of the Amazonian region believe tobacco originated in the mountainous headwaters of the Solimões River. They say wind-borne tobacco smoke created the Içana River's serpentine path. For the nearby Tukanonan people, the Grandmother of the Universe created people by chanting spells and blowing tobacco smoke over a gourd of sweet *kana* berries, producing seven "Universe People." The shaman of the Warao people in the Orinoco Delta of Venezuela is thought to spiritually ascend to the apex of the world, to an egg-shaped house made of tobacco smoke, formed by the creator bird of dawn.

The 'Big Reed'

The world tree is not always a tree. In Arizona, the first Hopi village was named Place of the Reeds, resulting from a creation story where only a virtuous few survived a great flood by climbing up a "big reed" (the Milky Way) that pierced the sky into the next world. The Hopi once intensively harvested a sweet, whiteish substance from common reeds along the Little Colorado River. The substance was an exudate produced by aphids, described by a priest in a Spanish mission. "It is a little less white than sugar but has all the sweetness of it." Hopi women were married and (ultimately) buried in the same dress of reeds. The ecological context and religious significance of an additional 14 world trees are explored in the appendix.

Chapter 8

The Seasons of Sex, Death & Rebirth

As the sun climbs higher in the sky and the frost lifts from the earth, great flocks of migratory birds arrive with spring thunderstorms. The rising groundwater chases toads and snakes from their subterranean winter homes as the first buds and tendrils emerge. It's the beginning of mating season for virtually every animal living in a riverine ecosystem.

The Pawnee celebrated the First Thunder of spring when the Swimming Ducks and The Snake in the Scorpio constellation began rising together close to the Milky Way on the southeast horizon. For most Native American tribes, the Thunderbird is a migratory raptor arriving in early spring with lightning striking from its beak and thunder rolling from its beating wings. The Choctaw of Mississippi describe a female Thunderbird laying eggs in clouds that fall toward the ground and crash against each other to create thunder. The male Thunderbird flies so fast trying to catch the eggs that he creates lightning. The way meteorologists describe lightning is not so different from the Choctaw version.

When ice crystals collide in a thundercloud, they form hail that grows larger and heavier until it falls toward earth, colliding with more ice crystals on the way down. The collisions pull electrons out of the ice crystals and into the falling hail, creating a massive negative charge at the bottom of the thundercloud. Without their electrons, the positively charged ice crystals float to the top of the cloud. The earth itself is positively charged, effectively creating an electron sandwich. When the two opposite charges touch, lightning explodes like a detonation cord, both inside the cloud and into the ground. Some ancient cultures believed that flint was created by lightning striking ordinary stone.

The sexuality of spring was sanctioned as a cultural norm and incorporated into the sacred calendar across the ancient world. It was no mistake that the season for human intercourse came at the same time farmers were watering and planting seeds in their fields. The Greek god of sexual license, Dionysus, was both son and husband to Demeter and Persephone, both goddesses of agriculture. In early Rome, a springtime procession honoring the fertility god Liber included large wooden phalluses carted through the fields. The festival ended in public intercourse between a priest and a noblewoman. The April celebration of Floralia in ancient Rome combined feasts of vegetation with ecstatic dance and sexual relations. Calling the rains, awakening the earth, and erotically evoking the universal power of fertility would today be described in academic terms as sympathetic magic.

Preceding the Greeks and Romans, the Egyptians held a public sex ritual every spring when drunkenness was allowed along with dancing and sex. The festival commemorated the sun god, Re, sending a catastrophic flood down the Nile, requiring Egypt to repopulate itself. In Mesopotamia, the Sumerians celebrated the springtime sexual union of Dumuzi and Inanna, the god and goddess of agriculture, with the king taking the part of Dumuzi and a high priestess representing Inanna in a chamber at the summit of the stone ziggurat (tower) in the center of the city. The state-sanctioned poetry describing the union was composed without inhibition.

I poured out grain from my womb,
at the king's lap stood the rising cedar
He shaped my loins with his fair hands
the shepherd Dumuzi filled my lap with cream and milk
he stroked my pubic hair, he watered my womb,
he laid his hands on my holy vulva,
he smothered my black boat with cream,

he quickened my narrow boat with milk,
he caressed me on the bed.
Now I will caress my high priest on the bed,
I will caress the faithful shepherd Dumuzi
I will caress his loins, the shepherdship of the land,
I will decree a sweet fate for him.

Early spring was the time of year for sex. During the Medieval Period in the French village of Carnac, men chased their naked wives around the ancient standing stones under a full moon. The only reason scholars are aware of this salacious activity is an order from a French king prohibiting the emission of semen at ancient sites. In Lyon, women seeking to get pregnant sat on heated stones known as *pierrefrite*. At St. Renan in Celtic Brittany, women slept for three nights on mysterious boulders known as mare stones. It seems the annual spring sex-fest spread to America, where in 1644 the Puritans banned May Day cavorting, which included young women of the village dancing around a pole and having sex in the newly planted fields. To encourage the crops.

The Time of Year for Death

Just as spring was the time for conception, autumn was the time of year when the calendar of the nature religions turned to death.

Thousands of years ago, life was short. Hunters died in accidents, women died in childbirth, and children died from disease. Rather than endure the repetitive trauma of holding a funeral for each death, some ancient cultures held a late autumn ceremony for the year's dead, when people would come from surrounding villages and gather at a sacred place to feast, dance, and sing, communally releasing the souls of their loved ones.

In cultures that lived by the rhythms of nature, it was common sense for the funeral gathering to be celebrated in late fall after the harvest was reaped, when the leaves were on the ground and the sun grew weaker every day. It was the time of year for death. British archaeologist Aubrey Burl wrote of Neolithic-era people in the British Isles traveling up to a hundred miles for a massive feast held in late autumn inside stone rings that ranged up to twenty-four acres in size, accommodating well over a thousand people. Burl cited the remains of hazelnuts, crabapples, and calves at various archeological sites to suggest an autumn date for the gatherings. The evidence makes one thing crystal clear: People ate more meat and drank more exotic beverages far more than they normally would.

The late-fall festivities would have coincided with the autumn bird migration, perfect timing for birds to carry away the souls of the dead. In late October and early November, whooper swans and other waterfowl gather in large flocks in the same pre-planned area, chosen for its safety and abundance of food, perhaps a shallow cove with plenty of algae. After a summer apart, whoopers engage in extensive and vocal greeting displays. After about 10 days of feasting on algae and mollusks, the entire whooper flock begins a remarkable song-and-dance routine that steadily accelerates in pace and volume, faster and faster until the birds take off on their migration. After observing the phenomenon, ornithologist Mark Brazil wrote that the calling and dancing appeared to be the whoopers' way to get psyched up for the long journey. After all it would be no easy task for whoopers to take flight following a 10-day feast. Brazil noted that whoopers weigh up to 25 pounds, placing them among the largest migratory birds in the world. Their wingspan is up to nine feet.

In the ancient past, when migratory birds were seen as soul guides to the afterlife, it's plausible that people imitated the gathering of bird flocks in late October and early November, right down to the feasting and dancing of the whooper, whose habitat touched much of the ancient world. At the end of the festivities our distant ancestors might have toasted the flocks that carried the souls of the year's dead beyond the distant horizon. A late fall celebration of soul flight could have been the foundation for what later evolved into the weeklong Celtic festival of Samhain, a time when the "veil" between the worlds was thin so souls could travel. The timing also coincides with Halloween and the Day of the Dead celebrations in Central and South America on October 31, when souls are said to be out and about.

The Tomb of Eagles

About 5,000 years ago, human bodies were left to be scavenged by white-tailed eagles before the bones were collected and buried in the Tomb of Eagles in the Orkney Islands of northern Scotland.

The remains of 342 people and more than a dozen white-tailed eagles were found in the tomb with human leg and arm bones neatly stacked. Human skulls were placed on stone shelves along the walls. For more than 500 years, the Tomb of Eagles functioned as a funerary site where unknown ceremonies were performed. Perhaps the ceremonies were also held in the last days of autumn, when the skies above the British Isles are filled with dozens of bird species coming and going in all cardinal directions.

The communal burial of bones was also practiced by Native Americans from Iowa to the East Coast, though it's unknown what time of year the rituals occurred. Along the Upper Mississippi River Valley at the Effigy Mounds National Monument in northeast Iowa are 31 mounds built in the shape of birds and bears, constructed between 800 and 1,600 years ago. About 25 percent of the mounds contained human remains. Archaeologists determined that the deceased were left outside until nothing remained but bones, which were bundled together with string and placed in a pit, often containing more than one skeleton. Scholars believe the effigy mounds may have been the site of communal ceremonies to connect people to their ancestors in the spirit world.

From Chesapeake Bay to Cape Cod, Native Americans left the bodies of the year's dead in trees or partially buried until only bones were left. In 1979, an ossuary was found on Indian Neck in Wellfleet, Massachusetts, an area where the shoreline is maximized by a series of coves and promontories. The ossuary contained the bones of 56 people of all ages and both sexes. Perhaps it was late fall in Wellfleet when Native Americans held the ceremonial burial 900 years ago, while hundreds of thousands of migratory shorebirds were taking off on their annual flight to South America.

The Time of Year for Rebirth

The winter solstice was the most important day of the year around the ancient world. It was the day when the sun miraculously stopped its death spiral and began its spring return. It would shine longer and rise higher in the sky for the next six months. The day was so important it was celebrated for an entire week.

The winter solstice was celebrated as the sun's birthday, the first day of its annual life cycle. Like any other birthday, it was a time to commemorate the sun's original birth, when light first appeared in the darkness at the beginning of time. People came from long distances to attend the festivities, expecting that the rebirth of the sun would infuse them with the divine energy necessary to heal their bodies and spirits. There was no doubt all the best musicians, dancers, and every healer in the region would be there.

In midwinter the walking paths alongside the rivers of China, Japan, Korea, and Vietnam were filled with solstice pilgrims enjoying the sweet-smelling white flowers of sacred plum and apricot trees still blooming in December, known as symbols of purity and perseverance. Across East Asia, plum syrup has long been used to cure sore throats and the tree's oblong leaves were boiled to produce an extract intended to clear the lungs.

Across western Europe, solstice trekkers would spot the distinctive green oval leaves of mistletoe climbing on oak and apple trees and stop to gather its winter-blooming white berries. Celtic tradition identified male sperm with mistletoe berries, which have long been used as a folk medicine to treat infertility, epilepsy, headaches, and arthritis. As they approached the megalithic temple, the travelers would have looked to the sky for the first sign of shooting stars from the weeklong Ursid Meteor showers, appearing from December 17 – 24.

An unusually high number of pregnant women at full term were among the solstice pilgrims, having conceived nine months earlier during the sex-fests held around the spring equinox. A communal practice of pregnancy would have created a group of women going through the same experiences at the same time, undoubtedly providing benefits to all involved. During the weeklong winter solstice gathering it's possible that pregnant women, infants, and even live births were somehow incorporated into the sacred ceremonies. For women at or near full-term, the walk to the sacred site and the drumming, singing, and dancing would likely have encouraged the onset of labor and the birthing process.

As the solstice pilgrims arrived at the sacred site, they saw the variety of wintering migratory birds along the river and felt welcomed by the light of bonfires and the smell of roasting wild cattle. Cooks used deer antlers to take glowing-hot quartz stones from firepits and drop them in kettles for heat. No one likes to cook around a lot of smoke. Depending on the region, emmer beer, maize beer or malt liquor was flowing and psychoactive plants from cannabis to mushrooms and cacti were consumed. For the first three days of the celebration, the communal focus was on waking up the dying sun.

Musicians frozen in stone at the Konârak sun temple in India.

Music, dancing, and poetry were part of evoking the sun's rebirth
in ancient legends of the winter solstice. When the Japanese sun
goddess Amaterasu hid herself in a cave in December, the other
gods came after her and built fires outside the cave, bringing with
them roosters that sang continuously. One of the gods danced on
an oval platform and laughed so hard that everyone laughed.

Amaterasu watched through a small opening in the cave and began to laugh herself. Then the gods made the opening in the cave wider and wider, and suddenly light filled the world. The roosters crowed and plants began to grow.

In a 3,000-year-old Vedic hymn, the Hindu goddess Usas is a radiantly beautiful woman who embodies the dawning of the sun. But Usas is tragically hidden in a cave on an island in a river at the end of the world, so with a troupe of poets and singers, the god Indra journeys to the cave and breaks through the entrance so the first dawn can light the world. A similar mythic tale is found in the 3,000-year-old Avestan texts of Iran, describing a hero who breaks into a cave where the sun is hiding.

From Cambodia to India and Egypt, musicians are frozen in stone at temples directly aligned to the winter solstice. The stone walls at Cambodia's Angkor Wat are sculpted with musicians playing double-headed drums, hour-glass drums, barrel drums, horns, gongs, chimes, cymbals, and conch shells. In India, the Sun Temple at Konârak features a dancing hall and sculpted musicians playing drums, flutes, lyres, and cymbals. At the Temple at Karnak in Egypt, court musicians play the sistrum (a rattle), harps, flutes, and tambourines. Throughout the longest night of the year, the bonfires burned amidst drumming, dancing, and singing, all to help awaken the sun for its annual regeneration.

In Greek myth, the sun gods Helios and Apollo held the reins of chariots, as did the Germanic Sol, the Hindu Surya, the Roman Sol Invictus, and the Norse goddess Sól. The horses pulling the chariots represented the raw power of the sun while the deity held the reigns, exercising the awesome power to turn the sun in its daily orbit. On the winter solstice, the responsibility of these solar deities was to stop the movement of the sun southward on the horizon by pulling on the horse's reins and turning the sun-chariot back north. Hindu texts describe Surya turning his chariot north on the winter solstice. During the last century of the Roman Empire, the Festival of Sol Invictus was celebrated on December 25 by holding three times the number of chariot races at Circus Maximus. Round and round the elliptical track went the chariots, covering 1,771 feet on the long axis and 262 feet on the short turn, encouraging the sun through sympathetic magic to turn its own corner towards spring.

Incubating Souls, Waiting for the Sun

Every megalithic temple designed to align with the dawning sun on the winter solstice was constructed where enormous flocks of migratory birds spend the winter, including some of the world's largest avian seasonal grounds.

Against the backdrop of wintering waterfowl and enormous megalithic temples gleaming with quartz and hammered gold, the sacred theater of the winter solstice told a supernatural story of the afterlife, of what happens between death and rebirth. The plot went something like this: In late October, migratory birds carry away the souls of the year's dead, flying beyond the horizon to a sacred wintering ground. The birds deliver the souls to a temple that is egg-shaped itself or has egg shaped design features, as a safe place for the souls to incubate and prepare for rebirth on hallowed grounds.

The climax of this ancient metaphysical plot occurred about six weeks after the birds delivered the souls to sacred ground. At the moment of dawn on the winter solstice, the first rays of the reborn sun lit up processional routes flanked by standing stones, blazed in the waters of southeast running rivers, were refracted into rainbow colors by slabs of quartz atop temples and monuments, and traveled down long, dark passages into the inner sanctum of megalithic mounds.

This was the moment everyone was waiting for, when the first golden beams of the sun's rebirth quickened the dormant, incubating souls of the dead to reincarnation and new life. The sacred calendar came full circle as the "new" souls took up residence in the many newborn infants that were present, or in the ovate bellies of women about to give birth. Eight ancient sites reviewed below share the major elements of the story: Prominent egg-shaped forms, a location on the winter grounds of migratory birds, a direct alignment to sunrise on the winter solstice, all designed at a time when the belief in reincarnation was nearly universal.

Clockwise from upper left are Brú na Bóinne in Ireland, Angkor Wat in Cambodia, the Ajanta Caves in India, and the Sleeping Lady inside the Hypogeum on the is land of Malta.

When whooper swans left Iceland in late fall to cross the North Atlantic, the ancient Icelanders believed the swans carried souls with them. The whooper flocks migrated to England and Ireland, with one large group spending the winter along the snaky River

Boyne and its serpentine tributaries in County Meath. The whoopers chose their wintering ground long before three megalithic mounds were built inside a sharp bend in the river more than 5,000 years ago. The flock, though considerably smaller, still returns today. Genetic evidence suggests the mounds were built by immigrant farmers who arrived from the Near East about 6,000 years ago. The slightly ovate Brú na Bóinne was designed so the dawning winter solstice sun would shine down a 60-foot passage and into a central chamber with a corbeled domed ceiling, among the oldest ever found intact. Thousands of smooth 'river-rolled' quartz stones that filled much of the mound were egg-shaped, about six inches across and nine inches long. Archaeologists believe the stones were gathered from a bay near the mouth of the Boyne, meaning a lot of work went into choosing them and bringing them back. Perhaps the egg-shaped stones were intended as temporary vessels for souls of the dead.

While the Celts didn't build the mounds, they adopted them and the visiting whooper swans as centerpieces of their mythological world. Brú na Bóinne was the home of the Tuatha Dé Danann (Tribe of Danu), who were known as "masters of rebirth" by the countryfolk of Ireland into the early 20th century. Mastering the discipline of rebirth meant being able to choose what family the soul would be born into next, similar to the practice outlined in The Tibetan Book of the Dead. Among the distinguished members of the Danann was Tuan MacCarell, who was said to survive Noah's flood by reincarnating as a salmon, then lived dozens more lifetimes and ultimately related the history of Ireland to St. Patrick.

The trio of Irish heroes, Lugh, Cuchulain, and Finn McCool, were all closely associated with Brú na Bóinne, and each was a master of every skill, presumably learned from living many lives. Cuchulain was miraculously conceived in Brú na Bóinne by the time-traveling Lugh and a flesh-and-blood woman, Dechtine. Finn was mentored by the River Boyne, where hazelnuts of wisdom dropped into the flowing waters. When the Tuatha Dé Danann were ultimately defeated by the invading Milesians from Spain, they agreed to surrender and disappear into the spirit world under the mounds and the waters. But an Irish legend suggests the Danann became spirits only to reincarnate themselves in the bellies of the Milesian princesses, growing up to be princes and kings, to once again rule the land. This nifty tale of conquest through self-directed reincarnation could also be interpreted as a more abstract expression of the Danann's cultural survival in their music, verse, metalwork, and artisanship.

The 6th century Welsh druid-poet Taliesin, wrote what appears to be a poem for children about reincarnation, this is a modern rendering: "First I was a fish and learned how to swim ... Then I was a whale and learned how to sing ... Then I was a bird and learned how to fly ... Then I was a wolf and learned how to howl ... Then I was a bear and learned how to sleep all winter ... Then I was an owl and learned how to spy my prey ... Then I was a rabbit and learned how to turn white in winter ... Then I was a rooster and learned how to tell time ... Then I was a bee and learned how to work for a queen ... Then I was a seagull and learned how to unwrap my lunch ... Then I was a giant clam and learned how to bury myself in the sand ... Then I was a turtle and learned how to make my own house ... Then I was a salmon and learned how to find my way home ... Then I was a penguin and learned how to walk upright, sort of ... Then I was an elephant and learned how to cool down my friends on a hot day ... Then I was a cat and learned how to chase dogs ... Then I was a dog and learned how to chase cats ... Then I was a horseshoe crab and learned how to swim upside down ... Then I was a kangaroo and learned how to carry things with me ... Then I was a snake and learned how to scare away other animals ... Then I was a bat and learned how to sleep upside down ... Then I was a dolphin and I learned how to play..."

Tonle Sap Lake in Cambodia is one of the largest wintering grounds for migratory birds in Southeast Asia. Just a few miles away, the ovoid conical towers at Angkor Wat represent the mythical Mount Meru, where Hindu souls are reincarnated. On the walls of the temple is the mythical Garuda bird, who discusses the metaphysics of reincarnation in the Garuda Purana. A wide canal forms a rectangle around the temple, attracting tens of thousands of birds. A small temple on a nearby hill was the designated viewpoint for watching the winter solstice sun rise over the towers.

In Maharashtra, India, the Ajanta Caves were dug out from a massive U-shaped rock face near the Jaikwadi Bird Sanctuary, a winter ground for about 30 species of migratory birds. On the winter solstice, Cave 19 receives the dawning sun, which shines on a standing Buddha, who appears to be emerging from a white egg of polished stone. The caves were built about 2,100 years ago, only a few centuries after the Buddha's death.

On the island of Malta, a popular destination for migratory birds on the Mediterranean/Black Sea Flyway, a three-level underground tomb known as the Hypogeum was built about 6,000 years ago, staying in use for 1,200 years. Archaeologists found the bones of about 7,000 people in the complex. The design allowed sunlight to penetrate the second level into the Holy of Holies at dawn on the winter solstice. Also on the second level is a sculpted mother goddess known as the Sleeping Lady, whose body is made up of oval shapes, including her legs, arms, and head. A small percentage of the skulls found at the site were elongated into an ovate shape, the result of intentional skull deformation in infancy. The second level of the Hypogeum also features the oblong Oracle Chamber, with a corbeled dome. Inset in the floor is a V-shaped cavity that could have held water, suggesting the possibility of steam rituals, perhaps to enhance the room's impressive acoustic effects. A voice speaking at about 110 hertz into a small oval niche in the Oracle Room produces an eerie echo that radiates throughout the tomb.

The oval ring known as Almendres Cromlech near Evora, Portugal features 95 oval/almond-shaped stones up to 11 feet tall erected more than 6,000 years ago. Evora is one of three almond-growing regions in Portugal. In Greek and Persian myth, the almond tree was associated with rebirth, reawakening, and victory over death. A single standing stone almost 15 feet tall and three feet in diameter was found about a mile from the oval, forming a visual alignment with the rising sun on the winter solstice. Solstice-goers likely brought almonds harvested the summer before to make a sweet milky drink. The cromlech is the largest in Portugal and Spain, measuring 230 feet on the long axis and 130 feet on the short axis. Scholars believe it functioned as an observatory.

Perhaps the most unique solstice site in North America is the Great Serpent Mound in southeast Ohio, located where the Central and Atlantic Americas flyways converge in a narrow corridor south of the Great Lakes. The mound was likely built at least 2,000 years ago by the Adena culture, which believed in a mythic Thunderbird that ruled the sky and a great serpent that governed the earthly realm. The Great Serpent Mound is 1,300 feet long and three feet tall, aligned to both solstices and both equinoxes. The snake's mouth stretches around an egg-shaped mound. Built on a ridge high above the zig-zagging Ohio Brush Creek, the mound may have been part of a "magico-religious schema" to attract migratory raptors to descend on their adversary, the giant serpent. The egg in the mouth of the serpent appears to mirror the star-group at the mouth of the constellation Draco.

Serpent Mound
on high ridge

Ohio Brush Creek, southwestern Ohio

In the late 19th century, a similar serpent mound was described at Loch Nell in Scotland, also with a stone ring at the snake's head. The age of the Loch Nell mound is unknown, but another serpent mound found in 2007 during a highway project in Herefordshire, England, was estimated to be about 4,000 years old.

The main feature of the Great Zimbabwe Ruins is the oval-shaped Great Enclosure, the largest prehistoric stone structure south of the Sahara, located in a volcanic area near the convergence of three bird flyways, a rare occurrence. Believed to be built about 800 years ago by an unknown Bantu-speaking people, the enclosure's granite walls are 32 feet high. A gold furnace was found in a hill complex north of the enclosure, where soapstone birds were carved at the top of stone columns in a semi-circular temple. In a 2002 study, Richard Wade of the Nkwe Ridge Observatory in South Africa found that the three bright stars in Orion rise over three standing stone pillars on the morning of the winter solstice.

Located where a route of the Pacific Americas Flyway makes landfall on the coast of northern Peru, the boundary line of the 2,400-year-old village of Chankillo was an oval stone ring with concentric ovate walls, a civic plaza, and a cut-stone temple surrounded by houses. Above the village on a north-south running ridge are the Thirteen Towers of Chankillo, with the north end aligned to the summer solstice and the south end to the winter solstice.

The Solstice Mystery of Carnac, Karnak and Konârak

The megalithic structures at Carnac in France, Konârak in India, and the Temple at Karnak in Egypt are all located on the winter grounds of migratory birds and designed to receive the first beams of the dawning sun on the winter solstice. The trio of temples were built by different cultures on different continents over a period of about 5,000 years, yet they have nearly identical names.

On the coast of western France, the place-name Carnac translates as "mound of the mother goddess." The ancient Egyptian meaning of Karnak is lost, but means "window" in Egyptian Arabic, perhaps to welcome in the rising sun. In Sanskrit, Konârak means "sun in the southeast corner," a reference to the position of the sun at dawn on the winter solstice. Perhaps the names relate to the Zoroastrian word for rooster, kahrkarak. Another potentially relevant name could be Karaca Dağ, the shield volcano in eastern Turkey that's a prime candidate for the Sumerian Garden of Eden.

The oldest megalith in western Europe designed to capture the dawning winter solstice sun is the Cairn de Gavrinis in the village of Carnac on the northwest coast of France, where a route of the East Atlantic Flyway makes landfall. The mound is 20-feet high and was originally located on a plateau overlooking the joining of three rivers at the coast, until rising sea levels left it on an island overlooking the Gulf of Morbihan. The age of the cairn is unknown, but the evidence shows it was abandoned about 5,400 years ago. The pillars along the passage to the central chamber are still covered with intricate carvings that were once painted in a range of colors. When the cairn was discovered, the inner sanctum was empty, and no bones were found.

A winged sun disk was sculpted over the entrance to the Temple at Karnak near Luxor, signifying the portal to a sacred world. The temple was built next to the Nile, a popular north-south route for migratory birds on the Mediterranean/Black Sea Flyway. A shallow pool the size of a football field was built at the site for the Sacred Geese of Amun. The temple dates back more than 4,000 years and was aligned to both solstices. On December 21, the sun proceeds along a straight path between ever-narrowing stone statues for more than a thousand feet, finally entering the inner sanctum, once lighting up a golden statue of the sun god Amun-Ra, which has been lost.

On the Bay of Bengal in northeastern India's State of Odisha is the shallow but enormous Lake Chilika, the biggest wintering ground for migratory birds on the Indian subcontinent. Nearby is the Sun Temple at Konârak, built about 700 years ago and aligned to the dawning sun on the winter solstice. The remains of much older solstice temples have been found on the site. After shining down a long pathway between various structures, the solstice sun enters the inner sanctum, once illuminating a green chlorite statue of the sun god Surya, embedded with gems.

Souls in the Steam: Rituals of the Winter Solstice

Evidence from a variety of winter solstice temples suggests that steam, gems, and the refraction of light into rainbows were part of rituals held inside the inner sanctum on the winter solstice. Commonly found at ancient sites, quartz is highly efficient at retaining heat, making it perfect for saunas and sweat lodges. Many cultures equate steam with the soul or essence of life.

An Irish legend describes "nuts" of celestial wisdom dropping from trees into a sacred well. Perhaps the nuts symbolized quartz stones dropped in the water of three ceremonial granite basins in the central chamber at Brú na Bóinne. To create a sauna, the top of the central chamber can be sealed or unsealed by a moveable flat stone. A year-round spring still surfaces in the 60-foot passage. The massive Entrance Stone at Brú na Bóinne could be interpreted as an ancient sign for a sauna. The carving shows diamond-shapes with lines radiating outwards, perhaps symbolizing heat radiating from quartz. The radiating lines morph into spirals, possibly representing clouds of steam. A triple spiral or triskelion was etched in stone just above the basin in the back recess of the central chamber.

An Irish legend describes three princes who came to Brú na Bóinne to learn the wisdom of kings, a process that included fasting for three days in the darkness of the central chamber. Adding steam to the experience of fasting and sensory deprivation would be consistent with the spiritual practices of other cultures. Native Americans considered steam to be the healing essence of life. A Wichita legend describes a miraculous scene when a father pours water over the fire in his lodge and the steam that envelopes his family turns them into eagles that fly to the heavens. Native Americans are known to use antlers to bring hot stones into the sweat lodge, a practice that likely originated much earlier. When Brú na Bóinne was discovered in 1699, a single pair of antlers was found in the central chamber along with three large stone bowls.

The floor of the inner sanctum of the Sun Temple at Konârak in India slopes slightly to the north towards a drain, suggesting water was used during winter solstice ceremonies, perhaps to make steam. Ancient Egyptian texts describe the inner sanctuaries of their temples as "the genuine great sea of the first occasion," referring to the primordial sea of Nun. The pyramidal Benben stone was said to fall into the sea of Nun at Creation, similar to the Irish legend of hazel nuts falling into the mythical Well of Sergais. In ancient Egypt, elaborate saunas and bathhouses doubling as medical clinics. On the first floor were boiling vats, sending steam through vents to the second floor, where patients were rubbed down with a range of oils as they lay on massive slabs of stone drilled with holes to let the steam through. Some Native American tribes kept steam going around newborns for several days to protect the infant's health. It's plausible that during the winter solstice, some megalithic enclosures or nearby caves were used as saunas for newborns and/or the birthing process itself.

Smoke would also have been used for dramatic effect. About 5,100 years ago at Stonehenge, cremated bones were placed in 56 equidistant postholes forming a circle more than 100 yards across. If 56 cremations were carried out at the same time, the rising pillars of smoke forming a circle would have been a dramatic sight to behold, most likely accompanied by drums, music, and dance. Quite literally the smoke could have signified the ascension of souls. Archaeologists found that Native Americans in Wellfleet, Massachusetts, placed still-burning cremated remains at the bottom of a pit before final burial, suggesting the rising smoke was a desired effect.

Perfecting the Light

Mysterious steam rituals practiced in the dark inner sanctum may have included gemstones that reflected and refracted the winter solstice sun, lighting up the coiling steam with scattered beams of colored light. It would have been simple enough to strategically place a chunk of transparent quartz to refract the incoming sunbeams. Clear quartz could have been heated and placed in a basin of water to create steam and color simultaneously.

A green chlorite statue of the sun god Surya once stood

embedded with gems in the inner sanctum of the Sun Temple at Konârak, refracting colors in the dawning solstice sun. Hindu texts say that on the winter solstice, the sun god Surya symbolically turns his chariot north, and "wears a rainbow robe adorned with poetry." On the summer solstice at the 5,000-year-old burial mound at Bryn Celli Ddu in Wales, sunbeams shine on a quartz-rich refractive stone that glows and sparkles in subtle colors.

In Los Padres National Forest in southern California are several caves where Native Americans made holes for the sun to shine through on the winter or summer solstice, including a cave at Painted Rock in the high grasslands of the Sierra Madres. In 1978, a group of students placed a polished crystal in a small five-sided hole that Native Americans had cut out in the floor of the cave long before. They found that at dawn on the summer solstice, the sun shined through the hole in the cave and onto the crystal, illuminating the darkness with rainbows.

The use of refractive crystals was not limited to caves or inner chambers. Gemstones and quartz crystals were used to bathe the outdoor audience in colored light as well. The 19th century physicist and author Norman Lockyer wrote of an ancient solar ceremony in which a Hebrew high priest faced the dawning sun while wearing a bejeweled breastplate, refracting colored beams of light onto the congregation. As evidence, Lockyer cited Josephus, the 1st century Romano-Jewish historian, who wrote of a solar ceremony involving the bejeweled breastplate that was abandoned 200 years before his time. Josephus wrote that the lighting effects could be seen from a distance, describing "bright rays … being seen by those who were most remote…" Evidence of such breastplates has also been found in Sumerian, Babylonian, and Egyptian cultures. Being bathed in colored light would have a dramatic effect on the gathering, contributing to the kind of ecstatic spiritual experience that was a foundation of the nature religions.

Winter solstice temples were typically built at high elevations, receiving the dawn earlier than the countryside below. Rather than having a priest play the bejeweled intermediary between God and humanity, numerous ancient temples were topped with refractive crystal, allowing for a mass experience of refracted light. Perhaps the most impressive example is the Pyramid at Giza, originally topped with massive slabs of polished quartz crystal. Dating back 5,200 years, scholars believe the mound at *Brú na Bóinne* was originally covered in polished quartz.

When the Japanese sun goddess Amaterasu hid in her cave during the winter and the other gods came with musicians and singers to coax her out, the first thing they did was erect the "True Sakaki tree of the Heavenly Mt. Kagu" and decorate it with jewels and a mirror at the center. The mythic description suggests that refractive gems and mirrors may have played a role in Japanese winter solstice ceremonies.

A recent study found multiple summer and winter solstice alignments in the pools and gardens of the 42-acre Taj Mahal in Agra, India, where gemstones were inlaid in sandstone as part of its extensive series of floral artwork, including 46 different plant species. As the sun rises and sets, the inlaid gems refract sparkles of color amid the flowery images.

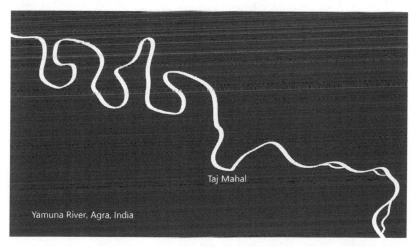

Taj Mahal

Yamuna River, Agra, India

Like gemstones, the use of steam may not have been limited to the inner sanctum. It is plausible that steam was used outside the temple in combination with colored light to mesmerize the audience at the moment of dawn. One of the more common features of megalithic sites are dozens of fire pits arranged in arcs or circles in front of the temple that could produce columns of smoke or steam. As the sun rose, gems could have been positioned to refract light through the coiling steam, all to frame the megalithic stage of drummers, musicians, and dancers, not unlike the light show and dry ice used by modern rock bands.

The Flight of Birds & New Year's Predictions

It would have been a simple matter to release a brace of doves from the entrance of a winter solstice temple to fly through coiling steam and rainbow colors, adding considerable drama to the moment of dawn. While this is sheer speculation, it would have been consistent with newly reincarnated souls emerged from incubation.

One thing is certain: As the ancient equivalent of New Year's Day, there was a lot of divination practiced on the winter solstice, probably including scrying (staring into still water) and tracking the flight of birds. In ancient Greece, public divination involved releasing a group of birds, then charting their flight paths and noting their landing places and interpreting the results to predict the future. If birds were released at dawn on the solstice, diviners could have observed where they chose to land and then publicly interpreted the implications for the future. For newborns arriving on the winter solstice, the arc of their heroic future lives might have been charted in front of a live audience.

From a design standpoint, sending birds out the front entrance of a temple could have occurred at Mnajdra and Ggantija on the island of Malta, the Cairn de Gavrinis in France, or *Brú na Bóinne* in Ireland, as each had a passage leading to an inner sanctum. The same display could have occurred using the mysterious vents at the Great Pyramid at Giza, one of which pointed directly at Cygnus when the pyramid was built. Archaeologists say the small shafts weren't needed for ventilation, and their purpose remains unknown. The one-square-foot vents are just large enough for doves to fly through and its opening is located high on the structure. From the vantage point of the crowds below, the birds would appear to fly directly out of the stone pyramid, displaying their ability to travel between worlds. Such an event would have been a dramatic, take-your-breath-away moment, a critically important aspect of the nature religions.

Halcyon Days: A Window for the Birth of Gods and Heroes

The full drama of the winter solstice could not be enjoyed in bad weather. On cloudy days, there would be no spectacle of the sun's first rays proceeding down a path or refracted in slabs of quartz. The weeklong Ursid meteor showers would be obscured by clouds.

Fortunately, a myth about the fictional Halcyon bird guarantees good weather during the weeklong solstice celebration. After a Greek sailor was lost at sea, his lover Alcyone threw herself into the ocean in grief. The gods took pity on them both and turned them into birds, but they required calm weather for the only week of the year they could lay eggs, between December 17th and the 21st. Luckily Alcyone's father Aeolus was the god of winds and made sure the weather was sunny for the "Halcyon" days.

Halcyon birds were not the only mythic beings that only gave birth around the winter solstice. The Greek author Plutarch wrote that the Egyptian Milky Way Goddess Net could only give birth on the last five days of the year. Murals of Net show her body covered with stars and bent over in the shape of an arch, her legs imitating the two southern "legs" of the Milky Way intersecting with the southeast horizon. Just after the winter solstice, Net gave birth to Osiris, Isis, Nephthys, Seth, and

Horus the Falcon, the spiritual liaison between the pharaohs and the sun god Re. In the Near East the pagan god Mithra was also said to be born around the winter solstice. Recalling the solstice myths of Japan, India, and Iran, the Koguryo of North Korea describe a river goddess shut away in a dark room until the rays of the sun cause her to conceive and give birth to an egg that hatched the first Koguryo king.

The first Roman emperor Caesar rebranded himself by taking on the name Augustus in 27 BCE, while officially associating himself with Capricorn and the miraculous regenerative power of the winter solstice. Although Caesar was a Libra, he made new coins with himself on one side and the December sign of Capricorn on the other. He also established six new towns with their main streets laid out as processionary paths for the sun on the winter solstice, including the town of Aosta. The mythic examples of solstice newborns growing up to be heroes, kings, and even gods would have been quite an incentive to copulate in the spring.

For hunter-gatherers, it was a common-sense adaptation (and an example of natural selection at work) for women to give birth while holed up in the middle of winter, a time when others could help them through the birthing process. When the group migrated in spring to work outside in their summer settlements, the infants would be mature enough to manage.

The Native American Winter Solstice

Massive stone temples in Africa, Europe, and Asia welcomed the rising sun on the winter solstice along a processional path and into a sacred inner sanctum. Native Americans built extensive earthworks east of the Mississippi River along with enormous sandstone communities in the Southwest, but none featured a solar processional path to an inner chamber.

The indigenous people of the Americas had their own style of celebrating the solstices, one that often involved unique vantage points and naturally occurring landscape features, sometimes augmented with rock art illuminated by the rising sun. In Peru people still gather for the winter solstice on the Island of the Sun on Titicaca Lake to watch the sun rise from behind a sacred rock. Across the western U.S., Native Americans found vantage points from which the winter solstice sun rose from between two mountain peaks, or directly out of a volcano.

At the top of Viejas Mountain just northeast of San Diego are the remains of a large ring once used by the Kumeyaay tribe to sing, dance, and watch the winter solstice sun rise directly over a local mountain peak. Each year the tribe climbed 4,100 feet to the top of what they called Song Dance Mountain to awaken the sun through the longest night of the year. There are at least 10 other well-documented archaeological sites in California where Native Americans once gathered to observe the winter solstice sun rising from a mountain or some other unique landscape formation. In other cases, the rising solstice sun produced a play of light and shadow across rock formations where Native Americans etched petroglyphs in the sandstone. In some cases, sunbeams move slowly over a mural-sized petroglyph to create an unfolding scene. At Fajada Butte near Chaco Canyon, New Mexico, the rising winter solstice sun creates two thin sunbeams that form a perfect bracket on either side of a spiral etched in sandstone.

Archaeologists have found that about 1,200 years ago regional gatherings at Chaco Canyon began drawing people from 150 villages as far as 155 miles away. Way stations were built every 18 miles along the 70 mile path south from Aztec Ruins. Bonfires were tended atop high buttes as beacons to winter solstice pilgrims. The solstice trekkers probably gathered winter-ripened juniper berries, some of the only sustenance available in the cold desert. Covered in white wax, the berries grow on red cedar trees, considered a world tree in the Southwest. About 170 miles northwest at Hovenweep is a six-room house with a porthole that welcomes the winter solstice sun, suggesting the event was celebrated at the family level. Anthropologist Frank Cushing reported that Zuni homes had the same solstice-aligned portholes.

The winter solstice occurs at a time of year when there are virtually no farming activities, yet scholars have long suggested it was identified and celebrated so farmers could track the seasons. This bit of speculation falls apart when considering that virtually none of the 50-plus California tribes were agricultural, yet they celebrated the winter solstice. Once inhabiting the coast near Malibu, the Chumash never farmed a field or ran livestock, but the evidence shows they celebrated the winter solstice. The day before the solstice/New Year's celebration, the Chumash settled their debts. Then they sank a feathered sun-stick into the earth, representing the axis of the universe, with dancers representing the rays of the sun, choreographically pulling the sun northward. After the solstice a high priest declared the sun was moving north again and proceeded to make predictions about weather and food supplies in the coming year. This was followed by dancing around sun-poles. At the Native American cities of Cahokia in east St. Louis and Poverty Point in northeastern Louisiana, massive rings of huge standing posts known as a "woodhenge" once marked the solstices and the equinoxes, much like the one at Durrington Walls near Stonehenge.

The Cosmic Archway

Ever since the Roman Empire made the arch a central feature of civic architecture, it has become a common site throughout the western world. Yet long before Rome was founded, the arch was a sacred shape in Neolithic Europe and later in the Americas, often encompassing a sacred place aligned to the winter solstice.

About 5,700 years ago, large U-shaped enclosures of stones began to appear in the Gulf of Morbihan on the western coast of France. Several more were built along the coast of Britain, and the east coast of Ireland. The open end of the U-shaped enclosures always faced east to the rising sun. Archaeologist Aubrey Burl wrote that people likely gathered inside these massive enclosures at certain times of year, such as the winter solstice, entering the open end of the horseshoe as they might enter a church. The U-shaped stone enclosure at Kergonan Ile-aux-Moines in Brittany was 210 feet wide and 285 feet long, capable of holding more than a thousand people. The tallest stones were placed around the closed end of the arch, which Burl believed was a sacred location for rituals. A container of sacred objects was found within the closed end of a U-shaped megalith at Achavanich, similar to the location of a modern altar.

In the Neolithic period, visitors to Stonehenge walked two miles from the snaking Avon River on a processionary path known as the Avenue to a vantage point just northeast, from which the dawning winter solstice sun appeared to bisect the U shape of free-standing trilithons at the center of the Stonehenge circle. The tallest of the trilithons is more than 23 feet high. Inside the U-shape was an oval ring of bluestones. The dawning winter solstice sun illuminated U-shaped recesses at the back of the chambers at Brú na Bóinne and the Maltese temples of Mnajdra and Gganlija. At the back of the solstice-aligned King Solomon's Temple, an arched doorway led to the Holy of Holies.

The arch was at the heart of sacred architecture in the Americas for more than 6,000 years. In the Chanduy Valley of southwest Ecuador, early farmers grew gourds (melons) along seasonal streams almost 12,000 years ago. There was no evidence of permanent settlement until about 7,000 years ago, when the U-shaped village of Real Alto was built atop one of the two highest points in the valley. About 60 people lived around a central plaza and buried the dead just outside their homes. About 5,000 years ago, more than 1,200 people were living in Real Alto, and the length of its elliptical layout had doubled. Residents lived in bigger, more permanent houses and buried the dead together inside one of two mounds in the central plaza.

The second mound showed clear signs of feasting, suggesting a communal funeral ceremony, perhaps similar to those held in Scotland at about the same time period, and the group burial practices of later Native American tribes.

Just south of Ecuador, U-shaped pyramid complexes began appearing about 4,000 years ago in northern and central Peru, just 500 years after the Pyramid at Giza was built. Archaeologists believe most of the regional population would have been needed to help build the megaliths, using river cobbles packed in fiber bags for fill. Twenty U-shaped temples were built in northern and central Peru, including the complex at Huaca La Florida in Rimac, which required 6.7 million person-days to construct. Unlike a pyramid in ancient Egypt, which was built as one project, the pyramids of ancient Peru grew over centuries with every burial. Under the corner of one structure was buried a four-year-old child whose eye-sockets were filled with shiny mica. A clear quartz stone was placed beneath the child's ribs in place of the heart.

Three-quarters of all Neolithic art is located in the Boyne Valley of County Meath, Ireland. Photo by Ben H. Gagnon.

About 3,600 years ago in northeastern Louisiana, Native Americans built a massive earthwork with U-shaped concentric ridges framing a 37-acre central plaza that backs up to the serpentine Bayou Macon. Each U-shaped ridge is 65 feet wide at the top with 75 feet between each one. Now known as Poverty Point, about 5,000 people once lived atop the ridges, enjoying beautiful views of the bayou. Most of the population would have been required to build the structures. At the summit of the biggest U-shaped ridge is the Bird Mound, the second tallest mound in the U.S. at 72 feet. Other notable examples of U-shaped forms in sacred settings include:

- The megalithic mound at Brú na Bóinne was built on a hill overlooking a sharp bend in the snaky River Boyne. Numerous kerbstones that ring the mound feature serpentine motifs. Also within the same bend of the Boyne are the mounds at Knowth and Dowth, with all three built more than 5,000 years ago.
- The Valley of the Kings is located within the largest, tightest U-shaped bend in the Nile River. Beginning about 3,600 years ago, the first tombs in the valley were oval-shaped and dug into the hillsides until space ran out and tombs were dug into the valley floor.
- There are no major rivers running through Jerusalem, but the Hinnom Valley to the west and the Kidron Valley to the east were once filled with water from the year-round Gihon Spring, forming a U shape of water that defined the southern boundary of the ancient city. Early settlers dried out the valleys by diverting water into channels leading to the city. Burial tombs dating back 3,000 years have been found at the confluence of the two valleys.
- Built at the top of a U-shaped bend in the River Ganges, the city of Varanasi has been the spiritual capital of India for more than 1,500 years, a place where millions of Hindus come to bath in the serpentine Ganges and purify themselves in one of the 2,000 temples along the river.

- On a high hill inside a U-shaped bend in the Yangon River, the Golden Pagoda of Yangon in Myanmar is 386 feet tall and dates back 2,500 years. It was covered in gold by King Mindon in 1871 and features thousands of gems.
- The Great Serpent Mound in Ohio was built on a ridge next to a sharp bend in Ohio Brush Creek. The rising and/or setting sun on the solstices and equinoxes bisect various U-shaped bends in the serpent.
- The confluence of the Anacostia and Potomac rivers was a major crossroads and trading center for Native American tribes long before Captain John Smith arrived in 1608. Congress approved a city map in 1793 and the U-shaped area between the confluence of the two rivers became the U.S. capital in 1800.
- At 5,900 feet in the mountains of San Augustin, Colombia, burial mounds 80 feet in diameter were built about 2,000 years ago on a flat area between two branches of the Magdalena River. A large U-shaped hill just north of the convergence also featured burial mounds.
- Built almost 3,000 years ago at 10,335 feet in the Central Andes, the Old Temple at Chavín de Huántar has a U-shaped central plaza open to the southeast. Its layout and location between two converging rivers that also form a U-shape is considered a model of the Chavin culture's cosmological beliefs.
- Three global bird flyways overlap in Mongolia, where the legendary Kublai Khan built the city of Xanadu in the 13th century next to a serpentine river. Italian physicist Amelia Carolina Sparavigna recently discovered that from the vantage point of the main palace at dawn on the winter solstice, the sun rose over one large U-shaped bastion in the eastern outer wall and set over another in the opposite outer wall.
- Ancient capital cities defined by U-shaped bends in

serpentine rivers include Paris, London, Berlin, Rome, Moscow, St. Petersburg, Berne, Krakow, Prague, Lhasa, Hanoi, Phnom Penh, Pyongyang, Perth, and most of the original capitals in the United States, from Concord to Nashville, St. Paul, and Sacramento.

If the arch form was so important, what did it represent? The appearance of the arch in so many natural forms may have been a factor. Its simple shape could represent the summit of a mountain, the bowl of the sky or an island in the sea. Another possible candidate is the Milky Way, which appears in the form of an arch in midwinter because of a visual illusion caused by its lower position in the sky.

The Rainbow: Connector of Worlds

The rainbow has long been symbolic of a doorway or portal between this world and the next.

The winged goddess Iris was described by the ancient Greeks as traveling on rainbows between the material and spirit worlds, to carry messages from the gods and bring water from the River Styx. In the ancient Turkic languages, the word for rainbow is bridge. Shamanic spirits were known to travel on rainbows produced by rock crystals. About 2,300 years ago, the Taoist poet Ch'u Yuan wrote of ascending to heaven by a rainbow. For South Sea Islanders, the rainbow was a heavenly ladder used by godlike ancestors. The Inca creation legend describes the first ancestors arriving in Cusco seeing a rainbow reaching to the mountains of the gods beyond.

A literalistic version of traveling to the sky via rainbow is found among the Aboriginal shaman of the Forrest River region in Australia. To initiate a student, the shaman put the initiate in a bag and literally pulled himself up the "rainbow serpent" to the top of the sky where the shaman let the initiate out of the bag. On an island surrounded by swans the student learned the secrets of medicinal plants and they both traveled back down to earth on the rainbow serpent. Shamanic figures across indigenous cultures played drums decorated with rainbows to call spirits to ceremonies. When a trained Navajo sings a cure for a patient, the verses guide spirits to another world on a rainbow, just as the gods' travel. "Swift and far I journey, swift upon the rainbow ... to life unending and beyond it, to joy unchanging and beyond it."

The Sumerian goddess Inanna was shown crowned with stars and wearing a rainbow necklace. In the days of solar worship, the ancient Hebrews prostrated themselves before the rainbow. Buddha was shown sitting on a rainbow in Bamiyan frescoes discovered in central Afghanistan. The Samoyed of Siberia say the rainbow is the hem of the cloak worn by the supreme being, Num.

The Neolithic Arch

Another natural phenomenon that may shed light on the U-shape in ancient cultures is the arching neck in the Draco constellation.

Just as dawn begins to break, the first bend of Draco is directly overhead, fading away in the growing light. As the sun sets, Draco reappears in the same spot, 90 degrees to the horizon. Seeing the same U shape of stars directly overhead at both dawn and sunset must have inspired awe and curiosity in ancient cultures. An observer might easily suspect a fundamental connection between the arch and the sun. In the symbolic language of ancient cultures, the shape of the arch may have reflected its position at the summit of the heavens. Perhaps the turning shape of Draco's arch was considered a heavenly sign of the power to turn the stars and the sun, to continue the immortal cycle of the universe.

Perhaps the importance of the arch was reflected by its manifestation in so many naturally occurring forms. The mountain summit, the U-shaped Milky Way in winter, the rainbow, and the arch of Draco may have reflected and embodied a belief in the continuous cycle of the universe, turning the corner from life to death, and from death back to life. Plato's advice was to nourish ourselves with the sublime qualities of beauty, wisdom, and goodness so our souls would "grow wings" and propel us to meet Zeus and a host of gods "at the summit of the arch of the heavens."

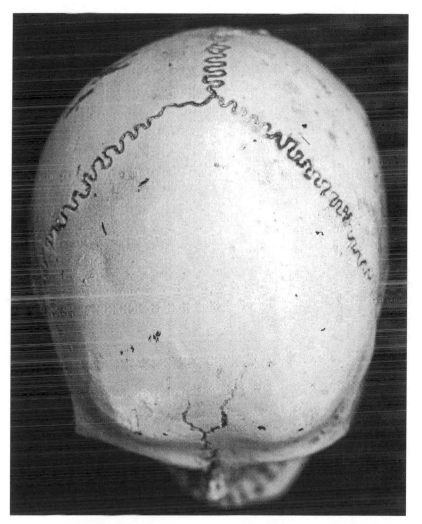

The snaky fibrous joints of the human skull.

Ancient cultures placed immeasurable value in the skull as the container of the soul. The ritual treatment and uses of human skulls were varied and widespread. It would not have gone unnoticed that the fibrous joints in human skulls form a U-shape, like snaky tributaries converging into a serpentine river. The form and shape of the fibrous joints would have been the ultimate microcosm, reflecting the riverine ecosystem where they lived. Perhaps they considered the U-shaped area at the front of the skull a sacred place where the spark of divinity resided. In modern terminology, the frontal area of the brain contains the cerebral cortex, also known as the seat of consciousness. From language to song, human vocalizations resonate in the bell-shaped space formed by the jaw, just below the cerebral cortex. Perhaps the people who attended winter solstice celebrations saw a link between the power of the rising sun on its birthday, the dawn of human consciousness, and the human voice raised in communal song.

The Promise of Spring

Why didn't our ancestors choose a date in early spring for New Year's Day? Shoots and tendrils are poking out, animals of every kind are awakening, and migratory birds are arriving.

The weeklong winter solstice celebration may have evolved by natural selection as a method to maintain the physical, psychological, emotional, and spiritual health of the community. As winter cold sets in and the days grow short, people can suffer from psychological problems linked to inactivity and/or a lack of sunlight. Internal conflicts may arise when snowy weather confines the group to a limited area. A midwinter mandate that people get outside and travel to the nearest megalith to spend a week singing, dancing, celebrating the birth of children, and reinforcing their shared beliefs about the universe may have been just what the doctor ordered. The winter solstice was a chance to physically move around, to see relatives and old friends, to consult one of the many healers in attendance, to eat and drink more than usual, to celebrate the deeds of ancient ancestors, and to welcome the birth of new heroes. Our distant ancestors latched onto the *only* tangible sign that winter would come to an end and turned it into the biggest festival of the year.

Chapter 9

Beckoning to Birds:
The Prayer of Geoglyphs

Geoglyphs are massive designs that can only be seen from high above, typically found at high altitudes and in large numbers. More than 300 geometric designs and 70 animals and plants make up the Nazca Lines in southern Peru, created about 2,000 years ago. Using drones, archaeologists discovered another 25 nearby in May 2018.

Amidst the chaotic social upheaval of 1968, Erich von Däniken's *Chariots of the Gods?* captured the imagination of a generation of young Baby Boomers by claiming that ancient astronauts from other galaxies used the Nazca Lines as an airfield. Despite being convicted for fraud and embezzlement the same year the book was published and serving a one-year term in a Swedish prison in 1970, Däniken's books have since sold 72 million copies. Over the last fifty years, the idea of paleocontact with extra-terrestrials has become mainstream. *Ancient Aliens* is now approaching its 20th season on The History Channel. Däniken and other self-described "ancient alien theorists" gather at AlienCon events in major U.S. cities, asking simple questions to which academics have no simple answer. Why were geoglyphs designed to be seen only from thousands of feet up in the air? Who were they made for? What was their purpose?

After fifty years of increasingly rampant pseudo-scientific speculation, bird migration mapping and the cross-cultural analysis of mythic stories have finally provided a clear and simple answer: The designs were created as part of an attempt to communicate with migrating birds that were thought to be divine messengers of the sun. Attempts to engage with deities were once common and are referred to by scholars as "magico-religious schema." The overwhelming majority of geoglyphs are found where two bird migration flyways overlap, typically on a plateau overlooking an ecosystem of snaky rivers and converging tributaries, the same bird-habitat that has attracted humans for countless millennia.

But the question remains: Why did people spend so much time and energy designing and constructing geoglyphs? What was their purpose? Considering the widespread ancient beliefs that birds delivered seeds to the landscape in spring and guided human souls through the spirit world in fall, our distant ancestors were highly motivated to attract migratory birds to their fields and sacred sites. Just a hundred years ago, the Bribri of Costa Rica danced on the fields in spring to attract migratory birds to drop their seeds.

Geoglyphs were likely part of a larger "schema" to engage with migratory birds that included drumming, singing, and dancing, usually on a plateau overlooking prime bird habitat. In 1586, Spaniard Luis de Monzon wrote that the Nazca Lines were made to honor the god Viracochas, who was expected to return as a great bird. A route of the Pacific Americas Flyway passes directly through the Nazca Lines, and most of the animal geoglyphs there are birds, one of the largest and most intricate depicts the sacred hummingbird. In the Americas, where most geoglyphs are found, most indigenous cultures believed the souls of ancestors returned as birds to help the living.

The Nazca Lines are etched in the desert next to extensive ancient watercourses with now-dry snaky segments and tributaries. A geoglyph depicting the Nazca world tree is located next to an ancient river system that appears much like the tree geoglyph. The branches of the dry river system create U-shapes that are clearly imitated on the tree geoglyph. As a symbol of water distribution, the Nazca tree geoglyph may have been associated with their system of underground aqueducts, a discovery reported in 2017 by the National Research Council in Rome. It seems the Nazca dug out spiral-shaped holes down to underground channels of groundwater and used wind power to establish and maintain a strong flow through the channels.

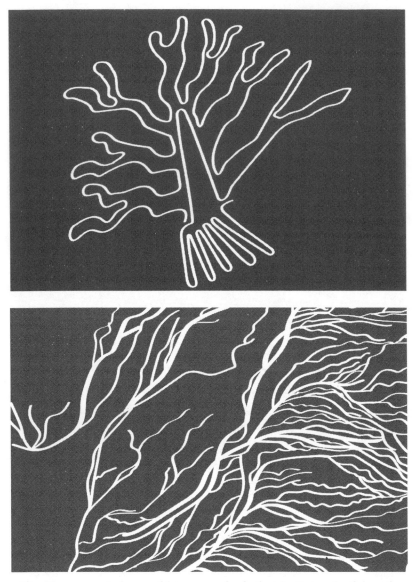

The Nazca created a world tree geoglyph that imitates the form of a dry river system located next to the geoglyph. The tree geoglyph is magnified so the forms can be compared.

The geoglyph known as Medicine Wheel was built about 700 years ago at the 9,600-foot summit of Bighorn Medicine Mountain in north-central Wyoming at the convergence of two global bird flyways. The view north from the summit overlooks a serpentine creek and tributary. A myth of the nearby Crow tribe tells of a boy with a burned face building the medicine wheel as part of a vision quest. The story goes that the boy drove away an animal that was attacking baby eaglets, and the mother eagle was so thankful it carried the boy to the sky and healed the burns on his face. The largest concentration of medicine wheels in North America can be found in Alberta, Canada, where the Pacific Americas and Central Americas flyways overlap.

In the arid desert of Blythe, California is a geoglyph in the shape of Kokopelli, a flute-playing deity that led the Hopi to their lands. Associated with fertility, satellite photos show the Kokopelli nestled among four ancient serpentine rivers side-by-side, each with multiple tributaries. In western Bolivia the Sajama Lines are a network of thousands of perfectly straight paths covering an area the size of New Jersey. The lines were created continuously over a period of 3,000 years ago near the Sajama volcano, where two bird migration flyways heading southeast turn due south. Recent studies have revealed that above-ground tombs or crypts were built at intervals along the Sajama Lines, which appear to connect various volcanoes in a network of sacred paths. In some cases, a line appears to end when it encounters a snaky river.

While most geoglyphs are found in the Americas, one was recently discovered in Kazakhstan by a Russian businessman playing with Google Earth. More than 250 geoglyphs have since been identified in the Turgai region, with their ages estimated between 2,500 and 8,000 years old. The geoglyphs are located where routes of the East Asia/East Africa and Central Asia/ South Asia flyways converge, including an extended segment of a snaking river.

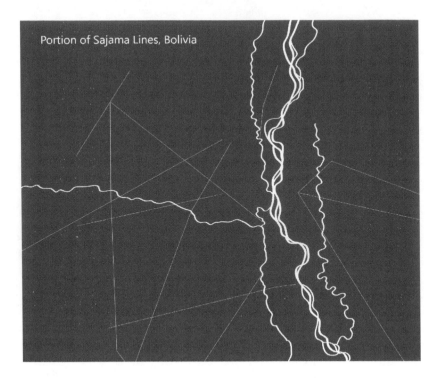

Portion of Sajama Lines, Bolivia

In New Mexico, the boundaries of two adjacent villages were laid out in the shape of birds that can only be seen from high above. Six hundred years ago, the Tiwa people designed Gran Quivira in the shape of a goose. Inside the boundary was a large city with rectangular pueblos and circular kivas spread over 611 acres. The largest pueblo had 226 rooms. Today, Gran Quivira is part of the Salinas Pueblo Missions National Monument. The National Park Service published a rare pun in the caption of an aerial photo on its website, noting the "bird's eye view." Not far northwest is the 90-acre Tiwa village of Quarai, including a large pueblo supported by year-round springs along serpentine Zapato Creek. Its boundary is in the shape of a songbird facing west, perhaps a mockingbird, which played the mythic role of conferring language on the different tribes.

Bird Sanctuaries of the Ancient World

Geoglyphs, serpent mounds, and bird-shaped village boundaries weren't the only attempts at interacting with migratory birds. Megalithic structures around the world commonly included water features and gardens, creating a mini-ecosystem favorable to birds.

The Temple at Karnak in Egypt featured a shallow pool bigger than a football field for the Sacred Geese of Amun, doubtless a peaceful place for the birds to rest and refuel. The City of Petra in the desert of Jordan was fed by a sacred well almost three miles away, transforming an arid landscape into a civic center with elaborate pools and gardens. A *NOVA* documentary dubbed Petra "the Las Vegas of its time" for the extensive water features. Located on a critical trade route, Petra's artificial ecosystem attracted migrating birds as an amenity for residents and business travelers. Greek and Roman temples featured pools, fountains, and gardens inhabited by domesticated waterfowl.

From a bird's eye view, the massive rectangular canals at Angkor Wat would be an unusual shape in any landscape, and in combination with planted gardens and adjacent rivers, a very inviting habitat for birds. Another large rectangle of water surrounds the Forbidden City in Beijing. It appears the concept was to draw birds down to the strange shapes reflecting in the sun and win them over with adjacent wetlands, fruit trees, and flower beds. Other sites that are hard to miss from above include the *Taj Mahal*, built in the early 17th century with a vast shallow pool and extensive gardens. The tomb complex was intended to be a cosmological model of paradise, with singing birds supplied from the nearby convergence of two flyways.

In Osaka, Japan, the 700-year-old tomb of Emperor Nintoku is located on an island in an artificial lake at a landfall of a route on the East Asia/Australasia Flyway. The site is 1,000 feet long with an island of green in the shape of a bell surrounded by water. In Ireland, Scotland, England and western France, more than 1,300 henges typically featured concentric circles of ditches once filled with water flashing in the sunlight. From a bird's eye view, henges would appear unnatural in the landscape, like the target of a dartboard. Perhaps the henge-builders hoped that sacred birds would identify water and be drawn to the odd shape.

The Dark Side of Däniken

During the fifty years since the release of *Chariots of the Gods?* critics have systematically accused Däniken of being careless in his research, citing a list of logical and factual errors. In 2005, author Jason Colavito accused him and other ancient alien theorists of racism in his book, *The Cult of Alien Gods*. "The underlying message of von Däniken's work has long been that non-white peoples are incapable of achieving great things without help from an outside force," Colavito wrote.

A similar phenomenon occurred in the early 18th century, when the insular world of English antiquarians speculated wildly about who built *Brú na Bóinne*, which was discovered accidentally by the site's new English owner in 1699. They started with the assumption that natives of Ireland could not have built a megalithic structure with a corbelled dome still intact after thousands of years, and speculated that the Phoenicians, Egyptians, or Danes had constructed it.

A similar debate broke out a century later in the U.S., where scholars and politicians insisted the massive burial mounds found all over the Midwest could not have been built by Indian tribes but must have been constructed by some earlier "civilized" nation that had likely been overrun by savages. One bold theory claimed the Atlanteans had built the mounds. As farmland was consuming the Native American burial structures, the Smithsonian Institution published a detailed book on them in 1849, providing a full record of the structures as they appeared at the time. The book professed not to speculate on who built the mounds, but suggested they were built by a more "civilized" pre-Indian culture.

Chapter 10

The Neanderthal Church of Birds

A trove of new evidence gathered across Europe and the Near East over the past decade suggests Neanderthals laid the foundations of the nature religions long before *Homo sapiens* emerged on the evolutionary tree. After the Neanderthal extinction, humans settled in the same volcanic areas where Neanderthals had lived and adopted their bird-related symbolic and ritual practices, described in Chapter 2.

Another symbolic practice shared by Neanderthals and modern humans was the use of red ocher at burial sites. Although ocher has been among the most widely used pigments in history, the source of its symbolic value remains mysterious. The most common rock containing red ocher pigment is hematitite, an iron-rich semi-precious stone that forms from magmatism and has the same physical appearance as obsidian. The symbolic power of red ocher may have been linked with red lava, the blood of the volcano god, and the awesome regenerative power of the earth. At Olorgesailie in Kenya, two pieces of ocher-rich rock were recently found to be "intentionally shaped" by early humans at about the same time the first obsidian trading network emerged in the region more than 300,000 years ago, according to George Washington University paleoanthropologist Alison Brooks, who identified the twin developments as "a radical shift in behavior."

More light may be shed on the subject by the unique bathing practices of the bearded vulture, which was among the six bird species from which Neanderthals harvested feathers for symbolic use. The bearded vulture is the only species that regularly stains its own feathers red by bathing in pools and springs rich in iron oxide/red ocher. After observing the bearded vulture staining itself red in a pool surrounded by volcanic rock, early humans may have "bio-mimetically" incorporated ocher into their rituals, as suggested by retired physicist Helmut Tributsch in a 2021 study published in *Animals*, an open-access, peer-reviewed journal. In the ancient world, vultures were believed to live for a hundred years and were perceived as divine agents in the regenerative process of sky burials and the migration of souls to heaven. Perhaps the use of red ocher in burials represented the fiery, passionate, and immortal blood of volcano gods intended to regenerate the souls of less perfect beings such as vultures and humans.

Ocher may have played a role in the emergence of abstract thinking. Overlooking the ocean on the coast of South Africa is Blombos Cave, where an early human used ocher to draw red crosshatching lines about 73,000 years ago. The grid has been identified as the oldest abstract drawing ever found, according to the University of Bergen in Norway. The meaning of the cross-hatching is unknown, but much later cross-cultural examples of the same pattern are thought by scholars to represent snakeskin, another symbol of regeneration. Recent studies have suggested that ocher was used as a sunscreen, insect repellent, adhesive, and a preservative for leather clothing.

A Robust Genetic Inheritance

Neanderthals first appeared in the fossil record about 430,000 years ago and have been found across Europe, the Near East, Central Asia, and the Melanesian Islands off the northeast coast of Australia. They were shorter than modern humans but had bigger skulls with larger noses, eyes, and brows. Their large facial blood supply gave them big, rosy cheeks. They were stocky with big hands and thick fingers, and stronger than modern humans. Some had brown hair and light brown skin while others had red hair and fair skin, which is more efficient at producing Vitamin D in weak northern sunlight. A series of genetic studies have revealed extensive interbreeding between Neanderthals and humans over tens of thousands of years.

Before 2010 scholars believed that if Neanderthals ever interbred with humans, it was for a brief period when they overlapped in Europe about 40,000 years ago. Today geneticists have traced the haplotype *B006* to confirm that extensive interbreeding took place between 80,000 and 50,000 years ago in multiple phases and locations. Using the language of scholarship, two recent books emphasized the amount of intercourse going on between Neanderthals and humans. "...these liaisons were not the exception but the rule, and they were essential for the rise of the often-variable and adaptable species that today we call *Homo sapiens*," according to Madeleine Boehme, author of *Ancient Bones: Unearthing the Astonishing New Story of How We Became Human*, published in 2020. Rebecca Wragg Sykes, author of *Kindred: Neanderthal Life, Love, Death and Art*, wrote that "... contact and hybridizing happened a lot more often than we'll probably ever know."

Recent discoveries at Nesher Ramla in Israel revealed a village of Neanderthal and archaic human hybrids thriving between 140,000 and 120,000 years ago. Located in the only volcanic region of the country, Nesher Ramla is north of Jerusalem in a region where two global migration flyways converge. Its settlers had "a distinctive combination of Neanderthal and archaic (human) features," according to a Tel Aviv University study published in the June 2021 issue of *Science.*

Much later, modern humans also interbred extensively with Neanderthals: A 35,000-year-old skull found at Peştera cu Oase in Romania has craniofacial attributes of both Neanderthals and modern humans. When geneticists examined large groups of Neanderthals and modern human they found as many differences within the groups as between them. Today the scientific name for Neanderthals is *Homo sapiens neanderthalensis*. We're *Homo sapiens sapiens*. Interbreeding over such a vast period of time was not likely the result of taboo sexual affairs, but of regular cohabitation in hunter-forager groups with shared beliefs and cultural norms. Having survived in Europe through numerous glacial periods over more than 400,000 years, Neanderthals likely passed on their hunting, cooking, and survival methods. It's likely that both archaic and modern humans had a deep appreciation and respect for Neanderthals.

A Very Human Portrait

A spate of recent archaeological studies is continually painting a more well-rounded picture of Neanderthal life. A 2017 reanalysis of bones found at Shanidar Cave in northern Iraq in 1957 found a male Neanderthal had lost a forearm, walked with a limp, and gone deaf at a young age but still lived into his 40s, suggesting a cooperative effort to care for him over an extended period. At sites all over Europe, the Near East, and Central Asia, Neanderthals adapted to their environment by eating a wide variety of plants and animals in different regions.

Fossils dated between 48,000 and 60,000 years old were found in Israel's Kebara Cave, where charred animal bones were the first reliable evidence of Neanderthal cooking. At Les Canalettes in France, they burned brown coal, which is hard to spark but radiates heat for extended periods.

- At Bajondillo rock shelter at Torremolinos in southern Spain, Neanderthals used heat to open 1,000 mussels.
- At Cova Negra and Bolomor caves in Spain, Neanderthals roasted 20 tortoises upside down in their own shells.
- Across 15 sites in the Mediterranean, Neanderthals primarily ate crabs and limpets.
- Between 43,000 and 48,000 years ago at Rio Secco in the Italian Alps, Neanderthals ambushed 30 bears that were either hibernating or waking up in a groggy state. There are 20 such bear-butchering sites across Europe.
- Evidence from fossils at Shanidar Cave shows that 40 percent of Neanderthals buried there ate boiled starches.

Similar evidence was found at El Sidrón in northern Spain.

• Between 300,000 and 337,000 years ago in Schoningen, Germany, Neanderthals made finely tapered wooden spears up to eight feet in length and used them to kill at least 50 wild horses.

Neanderthal butchering sites reveal expertise in smashing bones to remove the nutritious marrow and modern craftsmen would be impressed by their practice of carving the wood off-center for strength, weighting the tip like a javelin, and using the hardest stump wood for the tip of the spear. Neanderthals tanned hides, made string to sew together clothing and shell necklaces, and cooked bark to make tar and resins. The leg bone of a bear with five round holes corresponding to a musical scale was found in 1995 in Slovenia, suggesting Neanderthals made music. A subsequent study argued the holes were made by the teeth of a scavenging hyena.

Red Deer Bones, Headstones & a Skull Fetish

Starting about 120,000 years ago, almost half of all burials by Neanderthals and early humans in the Near East and Europe were infants and children, interred with substantially more artifacts and animal bones compared to adults. The death of a child clearly carried a unique and profound meaning for both Neanderthals and humans. The oldest human burial in Africa was excavated at Panga ya Saidi in southeastern Kenya, where a three-year-old child was carefully interred about 78,000 years ago with five large shell fragments of the spiral-shaped land snail *Achatina* near the back of its skull. When ancient cultures developed much later, myths described the souls of dead infants and children going straight to a heavenly place.

In 2002, a study released by the Instituto Português de Arqueologia described the burial of a four-year-old boy about

24,500 years ago at Lagar Velho, a rock-shelter near the northwest coast of Portugal. The boy was buried with the right pelvis of a red deer by his head and the left pelvis of the same deer by his feet. The deer bones were stained with ocher. About 70,000 years earlier and 2,500 miles away at Qafzeh Cave in Israel, Neanderthals buried the antlers of a red deer on the chest of a 13-year-old child. At nearby Amud Cave on the Sea of Galilee archaeologists found a Neanderthal infant buried between 50,000 and 70,000 years ago with the jawbone of a red deer resting on its pelvis. The specificity of placing red deer bones in physical contact with buried infants and children suggests a ritual practice shared by Neanderthals and modern humans over an astounding period of time.

At Shanidar Cave a more complete understanding of Neanderthal burials has recently emerged. The cave overlooks the Rowanduz River as it emerges from the Baradost Mountains and joins the snaky Greater Zab River, which flows into the Tigris. Shanidar Cave first made headlines when a 1960s study suggested Neanderthals buried their dead with flowers, according to pollen evidence. A later analysis challenged the conclusion, suggesting the pollen could have blown into the cave. The discovery in 2016 of more fossilized Neanderthal bones at Shanidar has helped fill in the picture of a "unique assemblage" of burials, suggesting Neanderthals returned to the same spot to bury their dead over time, according to a 2020 study at Cambridge University. "A prominent rock" was found next to the head of one skeleton, suggesting a possible marker to identify the deceased.

About 10,600 years ago, 35 people were buried at Shanidar Cave, all in the flexed or fetal position, with most clustered in an oval-shaped area. Slightly removed from the burial site were ovate sections of limestone pavement where archaeologists believe ritual burning took place. The bodies were buried in a layer of ash and charcoal, perhaps related to the volcanic region where the cave is located, but there was no sign of cremation (no bones were charred). The highest number and variety of grave goods were buried with infants and children, including spiral-shaped snail shells, colored calcite beads, and heat-cracked flint. A unique collection of wing bones was found at Zawi Chemi Shanidar, the settlement in the valley below, on the banks of the Greater Zab River. Similar to Neanderthal practice, the wings were removed mostly from bearded vultures, white-tailed sea eagles, and other eagle species, and were likely used in rituals. Also found at the settlement were tubular beads and a wing-shaped object made from bird bone, along with numerous ovate discs of white marble likely used as pendants.

A Passion for Precious Stones

Located where 940 migratory bird species converge on three global flyways, Mount Arteni in the volcanic Caucasus Mountains of Armenia is among the world's oldest and largest source of obsidian tools and artifacts, with examples dating back 1.4 million years. While the oldest obsidian tools were likely made by *Homo erectus*, most were made by Neanderthals and both archaic and modern humans. Artifacts number in the millions, according to archaeologist Boris Gasparyan of Armenia's National Institute of Archaeology and Ethnology. Mt. Arteni was still in the obsidian business about 3,000 years ago when tools were exported 1,600 miles away to Greece. Also located where three flyways converge, the volcanic Imereti region in the Southern Caucasus Mountains in the Republic of Georgia was a prime settlement area for Neanderthals and modern humans, who both produced obsidian artifacts along the snaky tributaries that feed the Kvirli River system. Neanderthals survived in the Imereti region longer than most other parts of Europe, finally disappearing about 27,000 years ago.

Early humans crafted obsidian tools where two bird flyways overlapped by an ancient lake 307,000 years ago at Olorgesailie in western Kenya, according to a 2018 archaeological study. Because the raw obsidian came from a source more than seventy miles away, archaeologists concluded it was the earliest trade network on record. In 2019, an obsidian mine was discovered at almost 11,500 feet in the volcanic Bale Mountains of southern Ethiopia, where two bird flyways overlap. The mine operated between 47,000 and 31,000 years ago.

Another obsidian trading network has been documented between eastern Russia and southern China about 50,000 years ago. Recent geochemical testing showed that obsidian artifacts found in Primorye, Russia originated more than 400 miles away near the Paektusan volcano in southern China, on the border of North Korea. Microblade cores were dated to between 50,000 and 2,500 years ago. The study also found a few artifacts near the volcano that originated in Primorye, suggesting a two-way trade.

Volcanic glass known as pitchstone was discovered about 5,800 years ago on the Isle of Arran in Scotland, where Neolithic people launched a trading network across the British Isles that lasted 400 years, according to a study by the University of Bradford, UK. More than 23,500 pitchstone blades and other artifacts were found at about 350 sites. Just 500 years ago in Mesoamerica, obsidian was known as Itzli, the god of stone, and was widely traded among the Aztec and Maya, who used obsidian blades in ritual human sacrifice.

Cannibalism or Ritual De-Fleshing?

Neanderthals sometimes dismembered dead bodies and removed the flesh, especially from skulls, leading some archaeologists to assume they engaged in cannibalistic practices. Others disagree.

De-fleshing may have been a ritualistic preparation of the dead, according to author Rebecca Wragg Sykes, who cited a scarcity of toothmarks on Neanderthal bones compared to frequent toothmarks in human cannibalism. At Moustier in France, the tongue and lower jaw of a Neanderthal teenager were removed, with the skull and lower jaw placed next to each other against a large flat stone, suggesting a ritual practice. Another Neanderthal skull was found with 35 roughly parallel cut marks from above the brow ridge, over the forehead and to the rear of the head, also suggesting a symbolic ritual. Humans have been known to remove flesh from skulls and dismember dead bodies in preparation for annual funeral rituals that focused on releasing the soul from the skull and bones. Along the Middle Awash River in Ethiopia, the fossilized bones of 12 early humans estimated to be about 157,000 years old showed cut marks consistent with removing flesh from the skull and at least one cheekbone. In one case, a hole at the base of a skull was polished and smoothed around the edges. More recently, skulls from the Neolithic era covered with plaster and polished sparkling calcite have been found in the Near East. In the region of *Göbekli Tepe* in southeastern Turkey extensive evidence has been found that villagers buried the dead beneath the home and then removed the skulls for some period of time, for some unknown purpose, before returning the skulls to their graves. The Natufians, who emerged in Israel and Syria about 15,000 years ago, also removed heads from the dead for unknown reasons.

Most ancient cultures perceived the soul as residing in the head, which may explain the ritualistic treatment of skulls after death, presumably to release the soul. Humans have also practiced dismemberment as part of a gathering of limb-bones for burial with and without skulls. At The Tomb of the Eagles in Scotland limb bones were stacked in square piles as part of an unknown ritual. Native Americans from the East Coast to the Midwest also arranged numerous limb bones together, sometimes collected in bundles, sometimes in stacks.

In summary, modern humans shared a number of Neanderthal practices, including 1) living in volcanic areas where two or more bird flyways converge, 2) creating symbolic oval forms in sacred settings, 3) using bird feathers and talons for ceremonial purposes, 4) the ritual treatment of skulls, 5) establishing ancestral graveyards, 6) burying animal remains with or near the dead, 7) heating stone or earth for ritual purposes, 8) using ocher as a red pigment, often associated with burials, 9) making tools from obsidian, and 10) making personal adornments of marine shells.

Mourning the Neanderthal

The results of radiocarbon dating at 40 Neanderthal sites from Spain to Russia were published in *Nature* in 2014, concluding that Neanderthals disappeared in Europe about 40,000 years ago. The results mean that *Homo sapiens* trekking north from Africa overlapped with Neanderthals in Europe for up to 10,000 years, depending on the location.

A 2016 study by the University of Cambridge published in the *American Journal of Anthropology* suggested the wave of humans from Africa carried herpes and other diseases, which may have played a role in the Neanderthal extinction. Without antibodies to protect them, the impact on Neanderthals would have been severe. The contributing factors behind the extinction have been debated for more than a century, but an equally interesting question is the impact on the surviving humans. How did they react to the extinction? The subsequent human adoption of Neanderthal rituals and symbols suggests humans identified closely with their departed cousins. It's likely that early humans had a profound respect for Neanderthals, and it's plausible their extinction was considered a tragedy that was widely mourned.

Post-Neanderthal Culture

Following the Neanderthal extinction, the Gravettian culture emerged more than 30,000 years ago across Europe, including the same volcanic regions of Germany, France, and Spain where Neanderthals had flourished.

The egg shape was common in Gravettian settlements at Predmost and Dolni Vestonice, Moravia, including oval homes, an elliptical burial pit, and figurines of the "Venus" mother goddess with over-sized egg-shaped hips and bellies. Other figurines created at the time across Europe included a category of bird-women, often with a bird head, a beak, and a female body.

Between 24,000 and 29,000 years ago, the related Pavlovian culture emerged in mountain valleys between southern Poland and Austria, where they used kilns to bake silt-loam figurines, apparently for ritual purposes, according to a study published in 2001 by Leiden University in the Netherlands. Pavlovian settlements were usually located near the confluence of a river and a smaller tributary, with a view of the valley below. The study found that Pavlovians lived in ovate dwelling and settled only in areas producing precious stones such as obsidian, chert, chalcedony, flint, and quartzites.

Neanderthals made personal adornments out of seashells about 95,000 years ago in the Near East. While there's no evidence of Neanderthals in Africa, shell jewelry was also made by humans 90,000 years ago in Nigeria, 82,000 years ago in Morocco, and 75,000 years ago in South Africa. Shell necklaces appeared in Europe about 50,000 years ago, and 41,000 years ago on the island of East Timor in Southeast Asia. It's impossible to say whether making seashell adornments was originally a Neanderthal practice shared with humans or whether it sprang up independently, or perhaps some of both. As for the Neanderthal use of ceremonial feathers and talons, the practice among human cultures was widespread in Asia and the Americas and is still ongoing in some indigenous cultures.

Cranial Deformation & the Cosmic Egg

The archaeological record shows cranial deformation began 12,000 to 10,000 years ago in the Near East, China, and southeast Australia, coinciding with the chaotic effects of post-Ice Age climate change.

Over time, intentionally shaping the heads of infants became a worldwide phenomenon found in Africa, Europe, Asia, Australia, and the Americas, typically in volcanic regions. In the Near East, archaeologists believe the practice of skull shaping began about 10,600 years ago in hunter-forager groups, using only the pressure of hands. Later techniques included boards wrapped around the head. Deformed skulls ranging in age from 5,000 to 12,000 years old were found in Heilongjiang Province and the adjacent Jilin Province in northeast China.

Scholars remain uncertain on the subject, but many believe the purpose of elongated skulls was to identify people belonging to families of high status. A 2018 study at Charité University Medicine Berlin found that elongated heads were a clear marker separating elites from the rest of the population. The study suggested that in times of regional conflict in the Colca Valley of Peru, efforts to negotiate were facilitated by the fact that elite groups on all sides had oval-shaped heads, establishing a common ground. Other studies have shown that cranial deformation among elite groups tends to coincide with greater social control, partly through the visual reinforcement of separate and distinct identities and societal roles. Recent forensic head reconstructions by French artist Elisabeth Daynès showed convincing evidence of intentional head shaping in the Egyptian royal family, but just for two generations, including only the controversial pharaoh Akhenaten, Nefertiti, and their three children. In Alsace, France, archaeologists found the ovoid skull of a woman of high status buried about 1,500 years ago.

While scholars have studied a range of physical methods once used to shape the cranium and the possible societal implications, the significance of the shape itself seems to be overlooked. The product of cranial deformation was typically an egg-shaped oval, the same shape as a Neanderthal or *Homo erectus* skull. Modern humans have round skulls, and those living in the Neolithic period may have believed that ancient knowledge was once contained in the oval-shaped heads of their own distant ancestors. An artificially oval head may have been the visible mark of a priest(ess), signifying a connection to ancient wisdom through sympathetic magic. Deformed skulls were found at Shanidar Cave, a Neanderthal burial site.

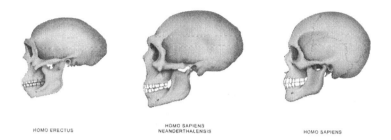

HOMO ERECTUS

HOMO SAPIENS
NEANDERTHALENSIS

HOMO SAPIENS

Similar oval-shaped skulls were found in China's Zoukhoudian Cave, where the remains of *Homo erectus pekinensis* were discovered. Coincidence? Is it possible the people of Neolithic China discovered the oval skulls of *Homo erectus pekinensis*, were understandably awed and impressed and proceeded to establish a head-shaping tradition that included burying those with deformed oval skulls in the same cave as their ancient ancestors?

While there's no evidence that Neanderthals made it to Australia, remains have been found on the Melanesian Islands off the northeast coast. Meanwhile, genetic analysis has shown the ancestors of Australian Aboriginals, who practiced cranial deformation almost 12,000 years ago, may have mated with an unknown human-like species in the distant past, according to a 2016 study published in *Nature.*

When the first evidence of cranial deformation appeared between 10,000 and 12,000 years ago, humans were living through a chaotic climatic period in which glaciers were melting, temperatures were shifting wildly, and normally predictable food sources were disrupted. Many scholars believe farming developed in response to the dislocated food chain. In times of chaos and dramatic change, cultures often take a reactionary turn to the past and embrace old and trusted traditions. Perhaps amidst the chaos and rapid change of the early Neolithic period, some groups manifested an existing adoration of the Neanderthal (and *Homo erectus* in China) by imitating the oval shape of their heads. An egg-shaped cranium may have been viewed as a vessel that ancient spirits could inhabit when called, bringing ancient wisdom to an unpredictable world.

Neanderthals and COVID-19
Up to 2.6 percent of the average European genome is made up of Neanderthal DNA, but that doesn't mean only 2.6 percent of Neanderthal genes survived.

Geneticists believe as much as 50 percent of the Neanderthal genome still appears in the human population in different combinations. For example, a Neanderthal gene that appears in one third of European women makes miscarriage less likely, according to a 2020 study authored by Hugo Zeberg of the Max Planck Institute for Evolutionary Anthropology. In the November 2020 issue of *Nature,* Zeberg's study identified a segment of the Neanderthal genome that increases the likelihood of serious illness or death from COVID-19 in 30 percent of the South Asian population, eight percent of Europeans, and four percent of Latin Americans.

Standing Tall
Some of the most important events in the deepest recesses of history are far beyond the reach of scientific tools. Yet it can be entertaining to speculate on the meager facts that are known.

Songbirds appeared about 33 million years ago in Australia, spreading around the world when the islands of Indonesia surfaced 10 million years later, allowing them to island-hop to Asia. Songbirds arrived in Africa about 22 million years ago and evolved for another 13 million years. The last songbirds to evolve in Africa were four species of warbler about nine million years ago.

The first primates emerged in Africa about 55 million years ago, but the first to walk on two feet emerged between six and seven million years ago. Standing tall at about three feet, *Sahelanthropus tchadensis* lived in southern Chad where three global bird flyways converge, encompassing almost 1,000 bird species. The second primate to stand up was *Australopithecus prometheus*, emerging about 3.7 million years ago in South Africa, also where three global flyways converge. The prevailing theory is that primates were motivated to stand up on two feet to reach the low hanging fruit in trees. A more recent notion suggests they stood up because it helped them cool down in the oppressive heat. In either case, why did it take almost 50 million years for primates to stand up and pick a peach, or cool themselves off?

Perhaps our curious primate ancestors were drawn to the bright colors and singing of a thousand migratory bird species flying around their heads every summer. The fact that millions of colorful birds came and went for six months at a time also must have inspired curiosity. Where did they go? Why did they come back? Would primates with a spark of human curiosity have an impulse to touch, grab or chase all the colorful, singing birds? Did the four species of warbler that evolved in Africa nine million years ago represent a tipping point? Perhaps primates dreamed of flying, as humans do. After all, to fly isn't just a romantic notion but reflects a desire for safety and security, high above the dangers of *terra firma*. Any observer of birds can see they stand on two legs, and waterfowl must run before they can take off. Was this inspiration enough for primates to stand up, walk, and run?

Chapter 11

Sacred Birds in Judaism, Christianity & Islam

*"No religion is completely new, no religious message
completely abolishes the past."*
– Mircea Eliade, Romanian historian (1907-1986).

Most scholars agree the Book of Genesis in the Hebrew Bible was written down starting about 3,400 years ago. The people of the time were familiar with the concept of a healing world tree growing in a heavenly garden, with divine birds in its higher branches and a serpent at the base.

While there were two world trees in the Garden of Eden, not a single bird is mentioned, a startling omission for the time. The talking serpent would have been another surprise, considering the gift of language was thought to be limited to people and birds. In the bird-less Garden of Eden, the serpent spoke to Adam and Eve and tempted them into breaking god's law, resulting in their being cast out of the garden.

The absence of birds in the Garden of Eden was a sign of perhaps the most shocking new idea introduced by Judaism, and later by Christianity, and Islam: There was to be no more reincarnation. In the trio of Abrahamic religions, people live only one lifetime, and their actions during that life are the basis for the eternal judgment of the soul. Gone were the long-beloved mythical roles played by birds carrying souls between the material and spirit worlds in the continual process of reincarnation. It was no accident that waterfowl previously considered soul guides were labeled in the Book of Leviticus as "abominations," and not to be eaten. The list of unclean birds was filled with previously sacred species such as eagles, vultures, ravens, swans, storks, herons, owls, and pelicans. Abandoning the cosmology of reincarnation also meant rejecting the divinity of the sun, the source of regenerative power that catalyzed the reincarnation of souls. In the Book of Genesis, the word "light" appears dozens of times but there isn't a single mention of the word "sun." Elohim is simply given credit for creating all the celestial bodies: "And God made two great lights, the greater light to rule the day, and the lesser light to rule the night. [He made] the stars also."

Yet as historian Mircea Eliade wrote, "no religion is completely new," and in the Hebrew Bible/Old Testament and the Qur'an, winged angels took on the mythical role once played by birds of intermediary between the earthly realm and the divine vault of heaven, bringing messages from the spirit world and carrying prayers to the supreme being. The word angel comes from the Greek word for messenger and the Old English word *aerendgast*, meaning errand-spirit. As birds once passed secret knowledge to kings and prophets, angels passed heavenly wisdom to Abraham, Noah, Daniel, Zechariah, and Enoch.

Like the sacred birds of nature religions, angels had knowledge of the future, brought the gift of language to humans, and taught them how to farm. In the Hebrew Bible, God descended from heaven with 70 angels to teach different language to the peoples of the earth. The archangel Michael later oversaw a process in which each tribe adopted the patron angel who taught them language. As winged gods taught the Sumerians how to farm, the archangel Michael taught Adam how to work the soil. Angels also served as guardians, always in close proximity to God (vigilant behavior is a primary characteristic of all bird species). Angels were sometimes ordered to follow and protect a man on an important mission.

The Hebrew Bible included the long-held common belief that birds delivered seeds. As a prophet-priest in Jerusalem and Lebanon, Ezekiel gave a great eagle credit for transplanting a vine, as described in Ezekiel 17. "A great eagle with powerful wings, long feathers and full plumage of varied colors came to Lebanon. Taking hold of the top of a cedar, he broke off its topmost shoot and carried it away to a land of merchants, where he planted it in a city of traders … by abundant water, and it sprouted and became a low, spreading vine."

It wouldn't have been easy to move the Israelites away from common beliefs in the sacredness of birds and the sun's divinity. About 2,800 years ago, before the Hebrew Bible was completed, the dawning winter solstice sun shined into the Holy of Holies at King Solomon's Temple in Jerusalem. Standing at the altar and facing both the congregation and the rising sun, the high priest was said to wear a breastplate studded with jewels, refracting rainbow-colored light onto the gathering.

While the adoption of the Hebrew Bible ended solar worship as a general rule, a related practice was featured in the Book of Exodus and survived in a new form all the way to the 20th century. In Exodus 28:15, God told Moses how to make a breastplate with 12 different "glowing (gem)stones" laid out in four rows of three. The breastplate was associated with two ancient Hebrew words: *urim*, meaning light, and *thummim*, meaning completeness or perfection. The concept may have been that white light from the sun passing through refractive gems is "perfected" into rainbow colors. The leading scholar on the breastplate, Dr. Cornelis Van Dam, believes it was meant to generate a miraculous light from God that contains a message. In the only known Hebrew ritual connected to the breastplate, congregants asked the high priest a yes or no question. After staring into the gems, the priest would answer yes or no.

The practice of manipulating white sunlight into colored light survived in sacred spaces in the form of stained glass across the Near East and Europe. The first production of colored glass dates back 2,700 years to Nineveh in northern Iraq. Mosques, palaces, and public spaces have long been decorated with stained glass throughout the Islamic world. Synagogues and churches also have a centuries-long tradition of using stained glass to heighten the spiritual experience of attending services. The first stained glass in

Europe appeared in Christian churches and monasteries in Britain about 1,300 years ago. Many churches are oriented east-west so the colored glass catches the light of the rising and setting sun.

In Israel's Abbell Synagogue at the Hadassah University Medical Center, the Jewish painter Marc Chagall created stained glass windows that were dedicated on February 6, 1962. The 12 window treatments were inspired by passages in the Bible, including the description of the high priest's gem-studded breastplate in Exodus 28:15. The colors of each section of windows, facing north, west, east, and south, corresponded to the rows of gemstones specified in the breastplate, including topaz, moonstone, sapphire, and amethyst.

The Volcanic Ten Commandments

The Israelites arrived at Mt. Sinai three months after escaping Egypt, setting the stage for one of the most well-known stories in history. As Moses gathered the people, the Hebrew god Elohim shook the ground and covered Mt. Sinai in a cloud. Scholars continue to debate whether the events at Mt. Sinai were volcanic in nature.

"There were peals of thunders and flashes of lightning, dense cloud on the mountain and a loud trumpet blast; the people in the camp were all terrified." Traditionally interpreted as a violent thunderstorm, some Biblical scholars point to the absence of wind and rain in the text to suggest Elohim's appearance coincided with a volcanic event, which typically produces thunder and lightning around the top of a volcano. As a reminder of Elohim's heavenly throne, the Talmud and Mishna say the Ten Commandments were etched in blue sapphire. Almost as difficult to cut as a diamond, the use of sapphire must have been strictly metaphysical: The choice makes more sense when considering sapphire is created by volcanic activity. Meanwhile scholars agree that Mt. Sinai and Mt. Horeb were two names used for the same mountain, and Horeb translates as "glowing heat."

With Mt. Sinai covered in clouds and lightning, the description of onlookers as "terrified" suggests something more than a thunderstorm. People were pretty tough in those days and weren't likely to be terrified by bad weather. But as God recited the Ten Commandments the people "trembled and stood at a distance." A distance from what? Imminent pyroclastic flow? Móses explained that God made the frightening display "so that the fear of Him may remain with you and keep you from sin." A powerful thunderstorm seems unlikely to cause the average person to upgrade their moral character, but surviving a volcanic event might do the trick.

Leading the Israelite's trek through the desert, Elohim appeared as a pillar of cloud by day and a pillar of fire by night. Clouds don't often appear in the form of a pillar unless they're shooting out of a volcano. Same for pillars of fire. Elohim dispatched the Egyptian army by using pillars of fire and cloud *at once*. "...the Lord looked unto the host of the Egyptians through the pillar of fire and of the cloud, and troubled the host of Egyptians, and took off their chariot wheels..." A pyroclastic flow would surely take off an army's chariot wheels.

Abraham's Oak and Aaron's Almond Tree

Judaism, Christianity, and Islam all trace their roots to the prophet Abraham, known as the Father of Religion. Legend has it that an oak tree grew on the spot where Abraham saw three winged angels as part of a religious epiphany in Hebron, Israel. Known as Abraham's Oak, the tree was alleged to be more than 5,000 years old when it died in 1996.

Etz Chaim is a common term in Judaism meaning "tree of life," and associated with wisdom in the Book of Proverbs. *Etz Chaim* is used to describe rabbinic literature and the synagogue itself. Known as the *Sefirot* in the Kaballic tradition, the tree of life reaches into the divine realms.

During the Israelite's long wandering in the desert, a group challenged whether Moses and Aaron were up to the task of finding a new homeland. Following God's directions, Moses asked the leaders of the 12 tribes to leave their staffs in the tabernacle overnight. The next morning the rod of Aaron had bloomed with the leaves, flowers, and nuts of an almond tree, demonstrating that Moses and Aaron were in God's favor. The spontaneous sprouting of Aaron's staff would have impressed those still enamored of the nature religions. The almond tree had been sacred long before the advent of Judaism, yet Elohim had produced one on demand.

Conception by Dove

Birds played important roles at several points in the life of Jesus, from conception to birth, baptism, and finally his crucifixion and resurrection. His conception and birth also track with the much older sacred calendar of solar religions.

In the biblical calendar, The Annunciation takes place on March 25, just a few days after the spring equinox, when the Angel Gabriel informs the Virgin Mary that she's about to conceive the son of God without the help of her husband Joseph. "The Holy Ghost shall come upon thee ... (and) that holy thing which shall be born of thee shall be called the Son of God." Paintings of The Annunciation often depict a dove hovering in a beam that shines on Mary. In some, there's a baby behind the dove and both are blown towards Mary by a wind from the mouth of God. The story of Christ's conception is not unlike the many cross-cultural creation stories claiming birds as divine ancestors. Nine months after The Annunciation, Jesus was born in Bethlehem on Dec. 25, four days after the winter solstice. A folktale from Normandy, France, describes a wren bringing moss and feathers as a coverlet for the infant.

The weeklong winter solstice celebration, from Dec. 17 to Dec. 24, was about the miraculous rebirth of the sun and its regenerative power catalyzing the immortal cycle of reincarnation. In modern terms, Christianity rebranded the winter solstice by celebrating the miraculous birth of the son of God, a healer who possessed regenerative power and promised an eternal life of the soul in the heavens. Under the Roman Empire, the sun god Sol Invictus oversaw 36 chariot races on December 25, the sun's birthday. But in 345 Pope Julius decreed that December 25 was the birthday of Christ. A 4th century mosaic found below Saint Peter's Basilica shows Christ holding the reins of a chariot drawn by four white horses, previously the role of Sol Invictus and other cross-cultural solar deities. During a Christmas Day sermon in the late 4th or early 5th century, St. Augustine made it clear that the sun was a creation of the Christian God. "Let us celebrate this day as a feast not for the sake of this sun, which is beheld by believers as much as by ourselves, but for the sake of Him who created the sun."

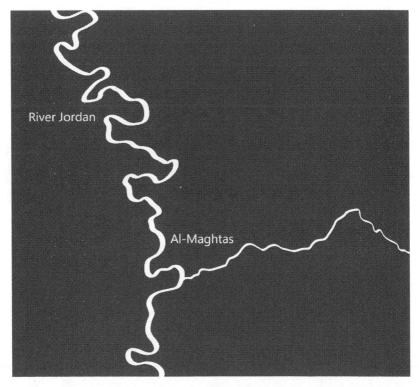

In the Gospel of John, John the Baptist sees "the Spirit descending from heaven like a dove, and it abode upon [Jesus] ... And I saw, and bare record that this is the Son of God." The site of Jesus' baptism has been celebrated for 1,600 years by the River Jordan at Al Maghtas, meaning "baptism" in Arabic. Al Maghtas was also the setting for a miraculous occasion in the Hebrew Bible's Book of Joshua, when high priests carried the Ark of the Covenant across the River Jordan, causing the river to part. A nearby mound known as Jabal Mar-Elias is the traditional site of the prophet Elijah's ascension to heaven.

After his baptism at age 33, the Holy Spirit overflowed from Jesus and he began to preach and heal the sick, attracting a large following. The powers of a great shaman appeared one night when Jesus and the disciples encountered a storm while crossing the Sea of Galilee. As the boat threatened to swamp, the disciples awoke Jesus who "rebuked the wind and said to the waves: 'Quiet! Be Still!'" As the sea grew calm, Jesus turned to his disciples and asked, "Why are you so afraid? Do you still have no faith?" The disciples had never seen him control the weather before, and asked each other, "Who is this? Even the wind and the waves obey him!"

The Tree of Immortal Life

A Christian legend describes a robin alighting on Jesus' bloodied head during the crucifixion, gently removing some of the thorns and staining its own breast with blood in the process, causing all robins to become red. (Is there a connection with the bearded vulture who cleansed itself with red ocher?) In nature the robin enjoys feasting on the hawthorn tree's red fruit in winter. Featuring thorns up to five inches long, the hawthorn tree blooms with flowers in late spring (around the crucifixion and resurrection). Christian legend says Joseph of Arimathea brought Jesus' wooden staff on a journey to England, where a hawthorn tree sprung from the rod during a rest stop at Wearyall

Hill, just southwest of Glastonbury.

During the Middle Ages robins were reported to fly into churches and sing in harmony with hymns while perched on lecterns, bibles, and choir lofts. The phenomenon inspired the satirical notion of the Bird Mass, described in the 1509 poem "Philip Sparrow." Gathered after the death of a sparrow killed by a cat, a robin led the birds of East Anglia in prayer. "And robin redbreast, He shall be the priest, The requiem mass to sing, softly warbling..."

The picture of a robin picking thorns from Christ's head while he perished on the cross resonates with a bird residing at the top of a tree or pillar, overseeing the process of death and the afterlife. Considering Christ's healing abilities and his promise to deliver souls to the heavens, pagans could have easily equated him with the tree of life. On Easter, Catholic priests certainly did.

- During an Easter sermon in the 3rd century, Hippolytus, the Bishop of Rome, said, "This tree, wide as the heavens itself ... is the fulcrum of all things."
- While St. Augustine was a bishop in Roman North Africa, he taught that the Christian tree of life was Jesus Christ.
- Saint Bonaventure, a 13th century Italian Franciscan and theologian, wrote that Christ was the medicinal fruit of the tree of life.
- Saint Albert the Great, a 13th century German Dominican friar, taught that the body and blood of Christ, as partaken at the Eucharist, was the fruit of the tree of life.
- In 2006, Pope Benedict XVI told a Palm Sunday audience in Sydney Australia, that the Cross of Jesus was the tree of life.

In the final chapter of the New Testament, the Book of Revelation promises that souls who reach paradise on Judgment Day will enjoy the healing benefits of the eternal tree of life. In

The Mythic Image, Joseph Campbell connected the Christian tree of life with the northern celestial pole, writing that the tree of life was "conceived as an axis extending vertically to the pole star and downward to some pivotal point in the abyss. Iconographically, it may be represented as a mountain, a stairway or ladder, a pole, or very commonly, a tree. It is symbolized in our Christmas tree, with the pivotal star at its summit, bounteous gifts appearing beneath..."

A 14th century fresco by Giusto de Menabuoi covering the dome of the Padua Baptistry shows Jesus at the celestial pole position, the highest central point. He is surrounded by "The Cloud of Witnesses," referring to the early Christian martyrs who were tortured and executed for testifying to their faith. Similar scenes reflecting the dome of the sky decorated the inner domes in numerous Christian churches.

Mysteries of the Cross

The Roman Empire crucified hundreds of thousands of people during its reign, mostly using stakes. After being mortally injured with iron-tipped whips, the victim may have been tied to a stake, impaled on a stake, or tied to a cross. The only remaining physical evidence of crucifixion is a human heel bone punctured from the side by a Roman nail, still containing a splinter of olive wood. A forensic examination suggested the victim was splayed out on an X-shaped cross.

In the early part of the 4th century, the largely pagan Roman population came to view crucifixion as a brutal practice. By 311, the Romans officially ended their anti-Christian campaign, and a year later the Roman Emperor Constantine fought the Battle of Milvian Bridge under the symbol of the Christian cross. The pagan Constantine reported hearing a voice in a dream that told him to "delineate the heavenly sign on the shields of his soldiers." When Constantine identified the cross as a "heavenly sign," pagans would have instantly interpreted the statement as an astronomical reference to the Northern Cross, also known as Cygnus.

Prior to that time, Christians never used the cross as a symbol, or Christ's death as a rallying point. For the first three centuries after the crucifixion, Christian art focused on Christ with a radiant halo, ministering to the sick. Even the most basic description of the cross itself does not appear in the gospels. It was Constantine and his dream that made the cross a popular symbol. Seeking to dampen religious conflict, the emperor may well have intended for the cross of Jesus to resonate with the pagan conception of the Northern Cross (near the celestial pole) as the ultimate destination of all who give their lives for the greater community. Direct ascension to the circumpolar stars for those who sacrificed their lives was a belief found in ancient Egyptian, Hindu, and Celtic traditions, and could be far older. It appears that Constantine's elevation of the cross as a symbol was a rebranding of Christ's crucifixion. The wooden cross Christ carried on his back represented both the burden of a martyr and his destination in the stars of the Northern Cross. Officially adopted in 325, the Christian Bible was said to be signed by the Holy Spirit in the form of a dove. In later Christian folktales, rooks were said to observe Ascension Day by pausing their normal activities such as building nests. Folk tales identified the blackbird as the guardian of purgatory, where souls did penance before their final ascension.

At least two Christian saints compared Jesus to the legendary Phoenix. In the late 4th century St. Ambrose of Milan wrote that the Phoenix "teaches us by its example to believe in the Resurrection." In the early 5th century St. Cyril of Alexandria wrote that God knew men would not believe Christ was resurrected and therefore provided the Phoenix as evidence that resurrection was possible. In the 14th century Bestiary of Philippe de Thaum, the Phoenix is compared to Jesus in that both had the power to die of their own will and return from death to life.

Christ's ability to transcend the material world was on

display when he glowed bright as lightning atop a mountain during The Transfiguration, when he learned from speaking with long-dead prophets that he would soon sacrifice his own life in Jerusalem. In the nature religions a shaman's apprentice is only able to ascend to the spiritual world of the heavens after he's been ritually dismembered or otherwise ritually slain.

Birds played pivotal roles in the stories of two saints martyred for professing their belief in Jesus. A dove was said to fly out of the mouth of a dead 13-year-old girl who was tortured and martyred in Barcelona in 303. She later became known as the virgin St. Eulalia and her story was reenacted in the eastern Pyrenees up to the 20th century. Also in 303, the young virgin Saint Devota was stoned to death by Romans for professing the Christian faith. Her body was saved and taken away in a boat and although a storm arose, a dove was said to appear and guide the boat to Monaco, to a church dedicated to St. George.

The stories of Jesus featured so many familiar symbols that it was easy for pagans to perceive him as a miraculously born healer, a preacher, and a prophet who could control the waters and guide souls to heaven in the circumpolar stars. Christ's emphasis on healing the poor and the sick resonates with the practice of the Yakut shaman of Siberia: "...(if) called at the same time by a poor and a rich man, go first to the poor." The wealthy, after all, have aid and support already in place.

Christianity later came to equate the molting and regrowth of peacock feathers in the spring with Christ's resurrection on Easter, a day when the Pope once traditionally waved ostrich feathers at the gathered crowds. Decorated ostrich eggs were symbolic of rebirth and purity and could once be found in Christian churches throughout the Middle East, Europe, and parts of Africa. In the 10th century, Christians adopted the egg as a symbol of Christ's resurrection, ultimately giving rise to the modern Easter egg.

Flying to Heaven with the Archangel Michael

In the early 4th century, the Emperor Constantine renamed the ancient city of Byzantium after himself. Constantinople is on a route of the Mediterranean/Black Sea Flyway that runs east-west, while birds spending the season to the north in the Black Sea use the Bosporus Strait as a north-south route. Every spring, Constantinople was alive with flocks of birds literally crossing overhead. While sleeping in a pagan church dedicated to healing and medicine, Constantine awoke to report a dream: The statue of a winged pagan deity outside the church had come to life and transformed into the Archangel Michael, who suggested he build the first Christian church on the site. In early Christian tradition the Archangel Michael weighed the soul after death, also a ritual practice of the ancient Egyptians. If the soul was light as a feather, Michael could fly the soul to heaven.

When archaeologists examined the remains of a 10-year-old child buried alone in a cave in the Kraków-Częstochowa Upland of Poland in the late 18th century, they were surprised to find the skull of a small finch in the child's mouth. The seemingly bizarre practice may have originated in the arcane world of medieval Christian symbolism, in which the image of a *dove* flying from the *mouth* of a saint represented the soul departing the body. Perhaps this iconic image was extended to the burial of an innocent child to guarantee its soul had a direct one-way ticket to heaven.

Constantine's vision of souls ascending to heaven on wings was a more pagan view of the afterlife than the Christian concept of the soul waiting for Judgment Day before (hopefully) ascending to heaven. In the first few centuries after the crucifixion, Christians believed Judgment Day was coming soon, so it wasn't much of an issue whether the soul went directly to heaven or waited a while. But with no Judgment Day in sight by the 14th century, a popular movement arose in favor of virtuous souls going directly to heaven after death, rather than waiting for Judgment Day. At first, Pope John XXII condemned the idea: "The soul separated from the body does not enjoy the vision of God which is its total reward and will not enjoy it prior to the resurrection [on Judgment Day]." Pope John's reaffirmation of this mandate was not well received, and he soon reversed course. The next pontiff, Pope Benedict XII, confirmed the new policy: If you live a life worthy of ascension, you will enter the gates of heaven upon death. No more waiting for Judgment Day.

The Rosicrucian Pelican

Emerging in the early 17th century, the secretive Order of the Rose Cross claimed to possess ancient wisdom handed down from a 15th century German mystic who made a pilgrimage to the Near East and returned with esoteric knowledge, including alchemy.

The symbol of the Rosicrucians was a rose at the center of a cross, often with a mother pelican piercing its own breast to feed its young with blood. The image was a mystical symbol of Christ's sacrifice and resurrection. The Rosicrucians rejected orthodoxy, dogma, and the cycle of sin and repentance embedded in the institutional church. They preferred instead the pursuit of mystical knowledge and personal spiritual enlightenment. Their favored Greek god was Hermes, whose divine traits match up neatly with the divine roles played by migratory birds in other cultures, including delivering seeds in spring, guiding souls through the afterlife, and acting as a messenger for the sun.

Wearing winged sandals and a winged hat, Hermes was the god of fertility and protector of vegetation, the conductor of the dead to Hades, and messenger of the gods. At a time when migratory birds were still thought to carry souls on a migration to the celestial pole and back, Hermes was the god of roads, travelers, doorways, and dreams. Birdsong was widely cited as the inspiration for human music, and commonly associated with flutes. Hermes was the patron of music, credited with inventing the lyre, and companion to the flute-playing Pan and his nymphs.

Flocks of birds were thought to gather in "conferences" to debate various issues. Hermes was the god of eloquence. Birds were commonly part of public divination rituals. Hermes presided over divination ceremonies.

Milky Way as Pilgrimage Path

In England, France, and Spain, the Milky Way's counterpart on earth coincided with Christian pilgrimage routes to sacred sites and early churches. In rural England, the Milky Way was known as Walsingham Way, the pilgrimage path to the shrine of Our Lady of Walsingham in coastal Norfolk County. In London, the Way of St. James was the earthly mirror of the Milky Way, following the serpentine River Thames to St. James Palace, built in the early 16th century. Just northwest of the palace is Serpentine Road. A sanctuary at nearby St. James Park, located on an island in the Thames, is home to numerous exotic birds. In France, the Path of St Jacques doubled as the Milky Way, snaking along the River Seine and leading to St. Jacques Tower, built by a masonic order in the early 16th century. The Spanish Path of Santiago appears to be a winding route across northern Spain from east to west, leading to the Cathedral of Santiago de Compostela, built in the early 9th century.

A common Christian legend describes God pouring out heaven's holy water, which froze into ice and was petrified by angels into a crystal form to protect and bless mankind. A strikingly similar myth can be found in southwest Australia, where the aboriginal Wiradjuri believed that the supreme being Baiame threw crystals to earth that were filled with "solidified light" from Baiame's eyes. The Wiradjuri supreme being was also known to sprinkle liquified quartz onto apprentice shamans.

Volcanos as Portals to Hell

In nature religions the earth sits atop a subterranean ocean from which water wells up to the surface in springs. The known earth was thought to be an island totally encircled by an ocean. All the waters circulating under and around the earth were part of the cosmic water cycle that extended beyond the horizon to the Milky Way. Cross-cultural mythology depicts spiritual seekers diving into a river or lake to enter the spirit world, sometimes accompanied by a spirit-guardian.

When St. Patrick came to Ireland in the 5th century, natural caves and the chambers inside megalithic mounds were sacred places, where springs burbled to the surface and fasting was combined with sensory deprivation in the pursuit of spiritual growth. Caves and artificial chambers were symbolic of the earth's womb, connected by the umbilical spring to the spirit world.

In Catholic legends of Ireland, St. Patrick battled grotesque serpents that emerged from once-sacred caves, including Station Island in Lough Derg, County Donegal, also known as St. Patrick's Purgatory. Emerging from a cave on the island, the serpent Caoranach swallowed St. Patrick, who slayed the beast by striking it from the inside with Jesus' staff. In another case, St. Patrick chased a she-dragon into a well in County Sligo. Considering that no snake species has ever been recorded in Ireland, the legend of St. Patrick banishing snakes was entirely symbolic, a proxy war against the nature religion's symbolic conception of snakes as guardians of divine waters.

Officially, there was no hell until after the Hekla volcano in Iceland erupted in 1104. Hearing of the volcanic event, Herbert the Abbot of Clairveaux in northeastern France declared two official portals to hell: One was inside the Hekla volcano, considered the eternal prison of Judas, and the other was in the Etna volcano on the east coast of Sicily, where hell was said to be visible from the crater's edge, with witnesses reportedly seeing the souls of the damned and hearing their screams. So began the centuries-long tradition of fire and brimstone preachers threatening the prospect of burning in hell for a life of unrepentant sin.

A Dialogue with St. Patrick

The demise of the nature religions and the rise of Christianity was captured in a speculative dialogue between St. Patrick and Ossian, a member of the *Tuatha Dé Danann* who had just returned from 300 years in the land of fairies to discover Christianity had all but taken over Ireland. A version of the dialogue is related in *History of Ireland; Critical and Philosophical, Vol. 1*, written by Standish O'Grady of County Cork, and published in 1881.

Ossian: Hateful to me is the sound of thy bells and the howling of thy lean clerics. There is no joy in your straight cells, there are no women among you, no cheerful music.

Patrick: O wretched old man and blasphemous, how shall I prevail against thy stubbornness and stupidity?

Ossian: Life is a burden to you, not a pleasure. Surely if the kingdom of heaven is made of men like you, (it would be) a wretched nation ... Where dwelled thy God, O lying priest, when we were in Erin? Surely had we known we would have conquered and bound him, surely, we would have burned his dun (house) with fire.

Patrick: It is not in fighting that my God delights but in causing the trees to grow and adorning the plains with grass and flowers. He loves not the proud warrior nor the hunter, but the lowly and the good. He abhors the feasting of the banquet hall.

Ossian: It was not in making flowers and grass my heroes took any joy, but in the cheerful combat of warriors and the loud-resounding chase, in practicing hospitality and speaking the truth, O prince of a lying race. You have practiced magic against the [Irish] ...Your hair, your glory of manhood, is shaven away, your eyes are leaden with much study, your flesh wasted with fasting and self-torture; your countenances sad; I hear no gleeful laughter, I see no eyes bright and glad, and ever the dismal bells keep ringing and mournful psalmody sounds. Not such, not such was our life, O cleric ... the music that I loved was that which filled the heart with joy, and gave light to the countenance, the song of the blackbird, the sound of the wind and thunder, the cry of the hounds let loose, the murmur of the stream and the ocean lashing at the shore. We did not weep and make mournful music. When we let our hounds loose, there was no doleful sound, nor when we mustered for battle, nor yet in our gentle intercourse with women — Alas! — nor in the banqueting hall with lights, feasting and drinking, while we hearkened to the chanting of noble tales and to the sound of the timpan and the harp.

Patrick: O thou silly old man, of whom I can get no good, if thou dost not cease praising the Fians, those pleasures innumerable that are in heaven thou shalt never enjoy.

Ossian: Now, by thy hand, O Patrick, come tell me, will the King of Grace be enraged if I bring my dog into his (heaven), or will he direct his servants to expel him?

Patrick: Thou stupid old man. He will not suffer thee to bring any quadruped into heaven.

A little-known oddity of St. Patrick's often legendary story was that he sought concessions from God for Ireland on Judgment Day. Apparently, God agreed to sink Ireland below the waves a week before Judgment Day to avoid the agonizing suffering that would be imposed under the reign of the anti-Christ. St. Patrick also asked for the right to sit in judgment of Irish people on Judgment Day rather than Jesus. Although God rebuffed St. Patrick's wish, he wouldn't give up on the idea. After a 40-day fast, St. Patrick had a vision of multi-colored birds, which he took as a sign that he won the concession.

Supernatural Birds of the Qur'an

From the Qur'an to classic Arab literature and Sufi poetry, the Islamic world has long recognized that birds have divine qualities and knowledge of the spirit world, which they conveyed to King Solomon and others in a secret language.

One of the holiest places in the Islamic world was made sacred when the angel Jibril (Gabriel) flew down from heaven and brushed the ground with one wing, causing a spring to well up in modern-day Mecca. Later, Allah instructed Ibrahim (Abraham) to build the Ka'bah where the angel's wing scraped the ground, known today as the Hajj or House of God. Jibril descended from heaven a second time to give Ibrahim the Black Stone, which he placed in the corner of the Ka'bah facing east, so it would sparkle in the rising sun. Every Muslim's pilgrimage to Mecca ends by circling the Ka'bah seven times in a counterclockwise direction, similar to the spiritually activating practice of circumambulation of mountains and trees found in other cultures. Some Muslim scholars believe circumambulation at the Hajj is somehow connected to the turning constellations in the night sky.

The Qur'an contains two passages in which birds play a central role in legends of resurrection and creation. In the first story, Ibrahim was curious about Allah's regenerative powers, and asked him, "Lord, show me how You give life to the dead." Allah instructed him to ritually sacrifice four birds and bury them in four hills. "[T]hen call them – they will come to you in haste." The second example is a story of Jesus that doesn't appear in the gospels, in which he demonstrates the power of Allah by creating birds from clay. "Indeed, I have come to you with a sign from your Lord in that I design for you from clay [that which is] like the form of a bird," Jesus said. "Then I breathe into it and it becomes a bird by permission of Allah. And I cure the blind and the leper, and I give life to the dead – by permission of Allah." In the Qur'an 16:79, the ability of birds to fly is offered as proof of god's existence.

Yet more bird miracles were coming, this time to protect Mecca and Muhammed himself. In 570, the year of Mohammed's birth, an Abyssinian invasion threatened to overrun Mecca until the city's defenders were joined by an enormous flock of swallows dropping small stones on the retreating Abyssinians: Mecca and the Ka'bah had been saved by the "Miracle of the Birds." At the age of 12, while working on a trading caravan, Mohammed was said to be followed by a cloud in the shape of a great bird, echoing stories of King Solomon traveling through the desert under a protective canopy of hovering birds. As the caravan approached Busra, the Christian monk Bahira saw the bird-cloud following it and concluded that a prophet was among the travelers. Bahira invited the company to a meal and upon meeting Mohammed told his uncle to protect the boy and leave him home next time. As the caravan moved on the cloud took its place over Mohammed's head again and was said to hover over him until the journey's end. Later in the prophet's life, birds again played a protective role.

After Mohammed fled persecution to Thawr cavern, it was said that a pair of rock doves began nesting at its mountain entrance, perhaps to alert him to danger. Islamic literature depicts birds as protectors, messengers, and symbols of the soul. In Arabic calligraphy spiritual words are drawn using the shapes of a bird's head, wing, back, or tail. A common theme of Sufi poetry is the mystical journey of the soul in the form of a bird. At the start of Farid al-Din Attar's 12th century epic, *The Conference of the Birds*, a hoopoe bird introduces himself to an avian gathering of many different species preparing for a journey. As a member of the "Celestial Army," the hoopoe says, "I know the Lord and the secrets of creation. When one carries, as I do, the name of God writ large upon its beak, one may be given the credit of knowing many a secret of the spiritual world." The hoopoe tells the gathering of their great bird king, the Simurg, "whose residence is behind Mount Caucasus."

In a challenging journey across seven valleys many birds lose faith, giving the hoopoe an opportunity to tell stories that strengthen their spiritual backbone. Several tales focus on the danger of becoming attached to transient things and worldly possessions. The nightingale discovers it must give up its precious roses to make the journey, and the owl must leave his domain as king of the night. Echoing with spiritual messages similar to those in Hinduism and Buddhism, the hoopoe says, "Gratification and disappointment of desires pertaining to the transient objects of this world are alike illusory. He cannot be said to be alive whose heart is attached to transient things." Just 30 birds survive the spiritual journey, only to fall into dust upon viewing a list of their earthly misdeeds. But like the Phoenix, a miraculous reincarnation emerges from the ashes. "After they had been thus completely purged and purified from all earthly elements, their souls were resuscitated by the light of His Majesty." The birds remembered nothing of their past lives as the sun rose before them. When the birds "cast furtive glances" at the "Celestial Simurg" they saw only themselves in reflection. The journey was over, and a measure of spiritual self-knowledge had been attained.

In Islamic culture, it was taught that birds should be treated with great respect. An 8th century ruler of the Islamic State named Umar ibn Abd al-Aziz, known as an educator and a pacifist, urged his people to tend to the well-being of birds. He wrote, "Spread wheat on the tops of mountains so it cannot be said that a bird went hungry in the land of the Muslims." It was reported that Muhammed once ordered a companion to return two young birds he had taken from their mother's nest. Beautifully crafted birdhouses were made between the 15th and 19th centuries by the Ottoman Turks, providing birds with safety and protection from the elements. Ostrich eggs once decorated mosques and were buried with the dead. When Imam Shakir Padshah died at Kaptar Mazzar in Turkestan trying to convert Buddhists to Islam, two doves were said to fly from his heart to become the ancestors of a flock of pigeons that populated the area. Up to the early 20th century Muslims were bound to stop at the pigeon shrine of Kaptar Mazzar.

The collection of ancient Arabic legends, known as *Arabian Nights*, includes a story filled with the iconography of birds and serpents. On Sinbad the Sailor's second voyage he discovered an island filled with brightly colored singing birds, murmuring streams, trees ripe with fruit, and rare flowers. Left behind by his crew, Sinbad climbed to the highest tree and spotted a giant bird descending to a nest of enormous white eggs, and recognized the gigantic creature as the Rukh, which was known to feed elephants to its young. When the massive bird fell asleep, Sinbad tied himself to one of its legs in a bid to escape the island. When the Rukh awoke it flew to incredible heights and landed on a high plateau, where Sinbad quietly escaped. Watching from a distance, Sinbad saw the Rukh grab a serpent in its talons and fly back toward the island. As Sinbad descended toward a valley, he came across a field of enormous diamonds guarded by sleeping serpents. He quietly took several diamonds and escaped by tying himself to a carcass until a gigantic vulture arrived and flew them both to a safe place.

The Sacredness of Jerusalem

Abraham was the father of the modern global religions of Judaism, Christianity, and Islam, and modern-day Israel is a sacred setting for each, most specifically the hotly disputed Dome of the Rock in Jerusalem. Is it a coincidence that 500 million migratory birds pass through the holiest place on earth twice a year, by far the greatest number of any country in the world? In the distant past, the population of birds flying through would have been much larger. Is it possible that the unique sacredness of Israel originated in the volcanism southwest of the Sea of Galilee and the seemingly miraculous number of birds that flew overhead?

Chapter 12

Eagles, Nations & the Fury of War

As divine agents of the sun, migratory birds delivered the seeds of vegetation in early spring and carried souls to the afterlife in late fall. The rank and file counted on their leaders to ensure that migratory birds kept their all-important schedule. Pharaohs and kings closely associated themselves with sacred birds, reassuring the people that the seasonal migration would continue, and both their crops and souls were in good hands.

Beginning about 8,000 years ago, the earliest kings of Egypt were known as Followers of Horus the falcon god, meaning the king possessed the divine ability to "follow" Horus, migrating to the heavens to be infused with the sun's regenerative qualities. Upon returning to earth, the king carried back the power to heal the sick. The tradition remained part of the later Egyptian dynasties, when the pharaoh was believed to transform his spirit into the high-flying falcon Horus, infusing himself with the self-regenerating qualities of the sun god, Re.

There were once temples to Horus all over Egypt, designed to replicate the lake and gardens of the afterlife, with falcon-headed statues in the inner sanctum. Egyptians visited temples of Horus to cure ailments, for the reading of omens, and for marital advice. The Temple at Edfu hosted the annual Coronation of the Sacred Falcon, when a real falcon was used to represent Horus. The ritual was intended to re-infuse the pharaoh with divine regenerative qualities. Crafted about 4,500 years ago, a black statue shows the pharaoh Khafre with Horus the falcon perched on his shoulders, facing forward to look over the top of the pharaoh's head, its wings protectively held out on either side. At the Temple at Karnak, an inscription describes Pharaoh Thutmose III transforming into a falcon and being infused with the sun god's divine qualities.

Horus protects the Pharaoh Khafre, who built
the Great Pyramid at Giza.

In ancient China, the Shang Dynasty began the royal mythic tradition of the Fenghuang, a Phoenix-like bird whose rare appearance foretold the death of an emperor and/or the ascent of his replacement. The latest appearance of the Fenghuang was said be in 1368 at the grave of the father of Hongwu, founder of the Ming Dynasty. In Hungary the mythic turul bird became a symbol of royalty and national identity about 1,150 years ago, when the first Hungarian king took the throne. The founding myth of the ensuing monarchy claimed that a turul bird appeared to the king's mother in a dream and told her a river would flow from her uterus into a foreign land. Just 600 years ago in Central Mexico, Aztec priests used a form of putty to make the king's nose look like a bird's beak and crowned him with a headdress of more than 400 bright green quetzal feathers to properly represent the feathered serpent Quetzalcoatl, who originally brought seeds to the Aztec.

As guardians of the royal lineage, sacred birds sometimes played the matchmaker. The Qur'an describes a hoopoe bird reporting to King Solomon about the beautiful Queen of Sheba and her prosperous land in southwestern Arabia. King Solomon wrote a letter for the hoopoe to carry to the queen, who ultimately brought gifts to King Solomon's court and converted to Islam. In the founding national epic of Ethiopia, King Solomon tricks the queen into intercourse, resulting in the birth of Menelik I, the legendary first king of Ethiopia, whose bloodlines ruled the land until the ascension of Hailie Selassie in 1924.

A similar story of bird-enabled royal matchmaking was told by the Greek historian Strabo, who heard it while traveling through Egypt about 2,000 years ago. "They tell the fabulous story that, when (a young woman) was bathing, an eagle snatched one of her sandals from her maid and carried it to Memphis, and while the king was administering justice in the open air, the eagle … flung the sandal into his lap; and the king, stirred both by the beautiful shape of the sandal and by the strangeness of the occurrence, sent men in all directions into the country in quest of the woman who wore the sandal; … she was brought up to Memphis [and] became the wife of the king." In 1812, *Grimms' Fairy Tales* included the same legend, which was later the basis for Walt Disney's *Cinderella* in 1950.

Myths from Greece to Ireland describe birds saving and caring for abandoned infants of gods or demi-gods, a plotline that may be based on an observable natural phenomenon. While whooper swans are unique in their permanent adoption of orphaned cygnets, many bird species that come across an abandoned chick get the attention of nearby birds by imitating the cry of the lost chick.

- After Phialo became pregnant by Hercules, her father, Alcimedon, put Phialo and her newborn son out of their cave and left them to starve. But a jay flew to Hercules, imitated the baby's cries, and led him to the rescue of mother and infant.

- Icarus threw his sinful daughter Penelope into the sea but she was saved and fed by widgeons. Seeing this auspicious event, Icarus relented and took Penelope back into the household.
- After the Assyrian goddess, Atargatis, abandoned her daughter, a group of doves arrived to feed the infant. She grew up to marry the king who founded Nineveh, outlived him, and built great monuments. When she died, she turned into a dove.
- An Irish legend describes a flock of birds attacking the castle of Emain Macha in County Armagh, making noise and eating vegetation. King Cormac's men chased them all the way to the Boyne Valley, where they discovered an abandoned infant in a hut who grew up to become the Irish hero Cuchulain.

National Birds

Across cultures and down through the millennia eagles have been symbols of national identity, military power, and elite warriors. Other species playing similar roles include the magpie shrike, hummingbirds, crested larks, and roosters.

Dating back 5,000 years, the emblem of the Sumerian city of Lagash was an eagle with wings outspread and its head to one side. About 3,300 years ago a double-headed eagle was sculpted on Hittite monuments at their capital of Hattusa, in modern-day Turkey. The double-eagle represented imperial Byzantium and the Roman army and later appeared on the Seljuk Turks' flag, and on coinage. The emblem spread to Eastern Europe, and became the imperial icon of Russia, Austria, Serbia, Poland, and Prussia. Perhaps like Janus, the two-headed eagle reflects the belief that birds have knowledge of all things, past and future. The eagle later became an emblem of knighthood in England, Scotland, France, and Italy, and appeared on the crest of cities across Europe.

Similar to the tradition of carrying a flag into battle, an "eagle-bearer" carrying a pole topped with an eagle effigy led each Roman Legion. The statue of a war-goddess near Rennes, Brittany shows a goose in attack mode on top of her helmet. In Ciumesti, Romania, a 2,300-year-old iron battle helmet was discovered with a bronze bird of prey on top. It was determined the wings once moved in the wind, perhaps to distract and/or intimidate opponents. The early Anglo-Saxons hung an eagle over conquered cities, a symbol of victory later adopted by Turkey, Austria, Germany, and Russia. No animal has appeared as a national emblem as often as raptors, which were depicted on coins, flags, and seals. There are almost 100 cities, states, and countries that have raptors on their official Coat of Arms. Other bird iconography includes:

- At Tell Brak in Syria, a vulture appears on seals estimated to be 5,900 years old.
- The eagle and the sun appeared on seals in Hittite, Assyrian, and Phoenician cultures.
- The Hindu Garuda bird (likely based on a golden eagle) is the national symbol of Thailand and Indonesia.
- The word Albania means "Land of the Eagles."
- In Kazakhstan, the steppe eagle adorns the national flag.
- In Africa, Zambia's flag is adorned with a fish eagle, Uganda's flag shows a grey-crowned crane, while Egypt's flag depicts Saladin's eagle.
- In the Americas, the Mexican flag shows an eagle devouring a serpent, and Ecuador's flag features a condor in flight.
- The Great Seal of the U.S. depicts a bald eagle. The U.S. Medal of Freedom is encircled by five gold eagles touching wings.

Devoted Christians saw a powerful parallel between the American Revolution and the Book of Exodus, when God freed the Israelite slaves from Egypt and led them to the promised land. In 1776, Benjamin Franklin and Thomas Jefferson recommended the Great Seal of the United States should depict a scene from Exodus. The proposal was rejected and the sensitive politics of church and state delayed the adoption of a Great Seal until Congress finally approved one in 1782. A bald eagle with outspread wings clutches arrows in one talon and olive branches in the other. From its mouth comes a Latin scroll, "E Pluribus Unum" or "out of many, one." Today, thanks to 24-hour eagle-cams, the nesting habits of bald eagles in Washington DC are being closely watched on-line. Nesting in the U.S. National Arboretum is a female bald eagle known as the First Lady, along with her partner, Mr. President. At a nest on the grounds of the D.C. Police Academy are another pair known as Liberty and Justice. In 2019, the news media reported widespread dismay among webcam observers when there were no eggs in either nest for the first time in 20 years.

The eagle wasn't the only bird associated with national identity and military might. After conquering France about 2,000 years ago, the Roman Empire established a new legion of fighters that bore the symbol of the Crested Lark, apparently because the lark was the herald of the morning, waking everyone to the task at hand. Much later under the first and second empires of Napoleon I and Napoleon III, the symbol of France was the Imperial eagle. However, the French Revolution of 1789 ushered in the Gallic rooster as the unofficial national symbol. The rooster was featured on the reverse of 20-franc gold pieces from 1899 to 1914, and at countless war memorials after World War I. Today there's a crowing rooster sculpture above the garden gate of the Palais de l'Elysée in Paris, the official residence of the French president. At soccer and rugby games, the crowing sound, "cocorico" is an expression of national pride. The rooster appeared as a mascot named Footix for the French team at the 1998 FIFA World Cup.

On the coast of northern France, the Counts of Bolougne once claimed descent from the Knight of the Swan, who mysteriously appeared and disappeared in a boat drawn by a swan. Duke Adolf of Cleves in western Germany also claimed a swan lineage. The privilege of keeping swans was once granted only by the royal families of Europe and every summer along certain stretches of the Thames, the "Queen's Swan Marker" still takes a survey of cygnets, a practice dating back at least 500 years.

Birds of War

The quick and brutal strike of a raptor on its prey was the source of inspiration for elite warriors from ancient Rome to Central Mexico. The efficiency of the raptor was impressive, but it was the mental ferocity that elite warriors sought to imitate. In Hindu mythology, the god Vishnu transformed into the two-headed eagle Gandaberunda when he needed an extra infusion of martial spirit. Warriors of the 19th century Zulu King Shaka wore the long tailfeathers of the magpie shrike, a black bird with a hooked beak that impales small prey on thorns. In southern Peru, Moche artwork showed hummingbirds with their long beaks, darting among the warriors.

A poetic glimpse of the dark inspiration once conjured for battle comes from the oral legends of ancient Ireland. When the war goddess Morrigan took her raven form, known as the Badb, she invited other dark powers to set the tone of battle: "And thus is described the meeting of the two armies at Clontarf, and all the hosts of the invisible world who were assembled to scatter confusion and revel in the bloodshed, and how above them in supremacy rose the Badb – a wild, impetuous, mad, inexorable, furious, dark, lacerating, merciless, combative, contentious Badb, which was shrieking and fluttering over their heads. And there arose all the satyrs and sprites and maniacs of the valleys, all the inciting phantoms. It was said that Murchadh set upon the invading Danes with a boiling terrible anger, an elevation of spirit and mind. A bird of valor and championship rose in him and fluttered over his head and on his breath."

North of the Great Lakes, the Ojibwe war song conveyed a similar determination:

Hear my voice ye warlike birds!
I prepare a feast for you to batten on;
I see you cross the enemy's lines;
Like you I shall go.
I wish the swiftness of your wings;
I wish the vengeance of your claws;
I muster my friends'
I follow your flight.

Chapter 13

Emptying Skies

From the viewpoint of an environmental reclamation engineer, the sacred groves of the ancient world were a highly effective method of maintaining a healthy ecosystem and clean water supply over the long term. Often located on the outskirts of a village, sacred groves typically featured a serpentine river running through them.

In Nigeria, a Yoruba legend recounts the voice of Osun the river goddess warning early settlers not to cut down her trees. The settlers heeded her warning and established the city of Osogbo on higher ground, while dedicating the forest to the river goddess. Today on the outskirts of Osogbo is the Osun Sacred Grove, with 40 shrines along a serpentine river that winds through protected tracts of dense forest. Traditional healers gather medicinal plants in the grove, but hunting, fishing, and farming are prohibited. Thousands attend the Osun Festival every August to celebrate the peaceful and enduring cohabitation of the Osogbo people and the Yoruba goddess. UNESCO made the Osun Sacred Grove a World Heritage site in 2005, citing it as one of the last intact examples of a once-common feature in African villages.

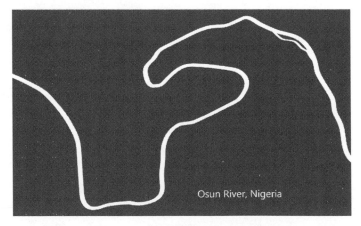

Osun River, Nigeria

In China a series of industrial, developmental, and cultural pressures have eroded the number and size of sacred groves and challenged the local belief systems that protected them. The flight of youth from rural to urban areas and the introduction of media communications technology has further weakened local cultures. A pilot project entitled, "Ethnic Eco-cultural Village" was launched by Yunnan University and the Ford Foundation in 2002 to bolster and reinforce the concept of sacred groves in southern China. In six villages across Yunnan Province, the project has helped the Sani people maintain sacred groves where they worship Mizhi, a god associated with protection, prosperity, and bountiful harvest. A festival culminating on the winter solstice is held each year between Nov 22 and Dec 22, emphasizing the ongoing guardianship of the groves and related laws and practices. A Villagers' Committee marked sacred sites and places of worship with wooden labels and built environmentally respectful pathways to connect the sites. They also established financial penalties for breaking rules in the grove. In 2005, the pilot project at Yuehu Village was among the first to be included in the Shilin county government's program of ethnic eco-cultural tourism.

A similar tradition of protecting sacred groves has been more successful across India, where about 14,000 sacred groves have been reported. The groves of India were established by Hindus, Buddhists, and Jains, complete with temples, shrines, and burial grounds. The *Vrikshayurveda*, a 10th century Hindu text, states that planting and raising trees is a karmic contribution to intergenerational balance. In the Hindu tradition, some sacred forests are off-limits to humans, reserved for plants and animals only. The sacred groves of India are associated with religious ceremonies, festivals, the planting and nurturing of trees, gathering herbal medicines, and recreation. The healing neem tree is planted in the scrub forests of the Thar Desert of Rajasthan. Ponds and streams inside the sacred groves are often used to meet local water needs, and many have become biodiversity hotspots, attracting animals seeking refuge from hunting and development. In 2002, India defined sacred groves as "community reserves" and provided protections through local governments, often assisted by non-profit agencies.

The Maya also had a practice of preserving sacred groves, as revealed in the Fall 2021 issue of *American Archaeology*. A recent study found the Maya had built around and preserved an area of rainforest when constructing the reservoir system at Tikal. Identified as a sacred grove by University of Cincinnati paleoethnobotanist David Lentz, the forest contains the ramon tree, which grows over 100 feet. Lentz said the modern Maya people create similar groves around their sacred sites. The shrines associated with sacred groves might be described as eco-churches, their open designs defined by a gentle embrace of the immediate environment, treading lightly on nature's creation.

- The ancient Greek legend associated with the Sacred Grove at Dodona describes a dove carrying the wisdom of the Egyptian pharaohs and settling in a grove of oak trees. To answer the questions of pilgrims seeking advice about the future, Dodona listened to the secret language of the cooing dove and rustling oak leaves, speaking together.
- The ancient site of Didyma in Turkey featured a sacred grove and spring where an unknown people built a walled enclosure, a well, an open-air sanctuary, a portico, and an altar between 2,800 and 2,600 years ago. The site was converted to a temple of Apollo about 2,550 years ago, when Didyma was the most important oracle site in Turkey, divining for the Lydian king Croesus and two centuries later for Alexander the Great.
- In the sacred grove of Ares at Kolkhis in Greece, the mythical golden fleece was nailed to the branches of an

oak tree and guarded by a giant serpent.

- At the ancient necropolis in Tarquinia, Italy, a fresco in the Hunting and Fishing Tomb shows a Dionysian dance in a sacred grove while another fresco shows birds on the wing.
- Névet woods is located in the only volcanic region of France, where Neanderthals once lived. Located in Celtic-dominated Brittany, the forest was a druid sanctuary now managed by the French National Forest Authority. The 560-acre site features oaks, birches, sweet chestnut trees, pear and other fruit trees, and evergreens.
- Tadasu no Mori is a 30-acre sacred grove located on the banks of the Kamo River near the convergence with the Takano River in Kyoto city, Japan. The forest was once believed to be a primeval, virgin grove that had never burned down. Now preserved as a national historical site, it's left to grow in its natural state; neither planted nor pruned.

A recent study suggests the greater diversity of bird life supported by sacred groves may have had a positive psychological effect. Living among a wide variety of bird species makes people happy, according to a study by the German Center for Integrative Biodiversity Research. Published in *Ecological Economics*, the study calculated that 14 additional bird species provided as much satisfaction to people as earning an additional $150 a month. Sometimes just one bird can inspire a local community. In Aberdeen, Scotland, a gull walked into a grocery store, grabbed a packet of tortilla chips, walked out, broke open the packet and ate the chips. The store manager became aggrieved when the practice continued, but local residents came to the rescue and committed to pay the store for the stolen chips. An increased interest in birding was one of many responses to the COVID-19 pandemic.

Death of the Sacred Grove

The once widespread religious tradition of conserving sacred groves declined dramatically as agriculture grew more intensive around the world. Over the centuries the often-swampy seasonal grounds of migratory birds were drained for farmland with the full knowledge that the soil beneath would be highly fertile from countless millennia of bird droppings.

When ancient cultures straightened serpentine creeks and rivers into squared-off canal systems, they destroyed a vast amount of fish habitat and unwittingly cut the connection between creeks and rivers and the groundwater below them. Breaking the link to groundwater meant the canals were deprived of minerals vital to the ecosystem. While canal building has long contributed to a decline in biodiversity, the more recent advent of mill-powered industry spilled toxins into rivers and creeks while the human population explosion claimed untold acres of land. Since 1500 a total of 161 bird species have been classified as extinct.

On September 22, 2019, the first five words of *The New York Times* story were disturbing: "The skies are emptying out."

The article was based on a study of bird populations in North America using 12 different databases and 140 NEXRAD weather radar stations across the United States to gauge the population levels of 529 bird species over a 50-year period. The Cornell University Lab of Ornithology partnered with the American Bird Conservancy, Smithsonian Conservation Biology Institute, U.S. Geological Survey, the Canadian Wildlife Service, and the National Audubon Society. The study found there are 2.9 billion fewer birds in North America compared to 1970, a decline of 25 percent. The biggest losses were in grassland regions where more than 700 million birds were lost since 1970, a decline of more than 50 percent. Hard-hit were warblers, sparrows, blackbirds, and finches. Many bird species in decline play vital ecological roles by controlling insects, pollinating flowers, and spreading seeds.

- Across the boreal forests of Canada, a decline of about 500 million birds since 1970 was reported, a drop of more than 30 percent.
- In the Eastern Forest of the U.S., 167 million birds have been lost, a 20 percent drop.
- In the Western Forest, including northern Mexico, about 140 million birds have disappeared, a nearly 30 percent decline.
- Melting permafrost in the Arctic tundra has contributed to a loss of about 80 million birds since 1970, a decline of about 20 percent.
- The number of birds in the American Southwest dropped by 35 million, or 15 percent.

The study found some good news in waterfowl populations, which increased by 34 million since 1970, and raptors, which rose by 15 million. The bird populations in wetlands also were found to increase by 20 million, or more than 10 percent. The study's authors believe these increases were due to the closer regulation of wetlands and the ban on DDT in 1972. While the study focused on population trends and not underlying causes, ornithologists believe birds have suffered habitat loss to human development, insecticides, declines in insect populations, oil and gas drilling, logging, shifting food sources due to climate change, increasingly large forest fires, outdoor cats, and glass skyscrapers.

"We're eating away at the foundations of all of our major ecosystems on the continent," said Arvind Panjabi of the Colorado-based Bird Conservancy of the Rockies, and co-author of the study. Although the declines have been dramatic over 50 years, they've also been gradual enough that each generation takes for granted how many birds are in the sky. The lead author of the study, Kenneth V. Rosenberg of Cornell University, found the results "staggering ... It's not just these highly threatened birds that we're afraid are going to go on the endangered species list. It's across the board." Rosenburg added a major effort to halt the decline in bird populations could turn things around, but warned, "that may not be true 10 years from now."

Similar disturbing population trends are being measured across the farming regions of France, including a decline in the common blackbird, according to Dr. Kevin Gaston of the University of Exeter. In Germany an 80 percent drop in the insect population over the last 40 years has been reported. It's likely that pesticides are responsible for the disappearance of insects, which has in turn deprived birds of a major food source, according to Benoit Fontaine, a conservation biologist at the National Museum of Natural History in Paris.

On the Indian subcontinent, the vulture population dropped by more than 97 percent in the late 20th and early 21st century due to a drug used on livestock that was poisonous to birds. Although the drug was banned in 2006, the damage was done. In 2001, the Parsi communities in India that practice sky burials were evaluating whether to breed captive vultures to do the job of consuming human bodies. Some have begun subgrade burials, threatening an ancient tradition.

Across China fewer than 3,000 Oriental storks remained in the wild as of 2018, officially making it an endangered species after years of poaching, habitat loss, and pollution. The stork's migratory stopover sites on China's east coast have been taken over by aquaculture fisheries, according to a study at Hebei Agricultural University in China, reported in the November 2020 issue of *Science*. Fishery workers have been reported throwing firecrackers at the storks.

With a wingspan of 10 feet, the Andean condor was once considered a sacred bird of the sun but is now listed as "globally vulnerable" due to illegal capture and shootings as well as the deliberate poisoning of carcasses by farmers seeking to kill mammals that they believe prey on livestock. Only a coordinated effort can help stop the decline, according to a study by the

University of Madrid referenced in the March 2021 issue of *Science*. Over the last century in Egypt the marbled duck, the white-headed duck and the ibis have disappeared, and the great crested grebe and white-tailed sea eagle no longer breed there. Vultures in Africa have been declining dramatically due to the illegal trade in their body parts.

As the official Red List Authority for birds, BirdLife International identified the sharpest decline in bird populations since 1988 as occurring in Asia, largely due to the rapid destruction of forests in Borneo and Sumatra in the 1990s. BirdLife also reported accelerated declines of open-ocean seabirds linked with the expansion of commercial longline fisheries and lists more than 1,400 bird species as globally threatened. Brazil and Indonesia have the highest numbers with 122 and 119 threatened bird species respectively. Nineteen bird species went extinct in the last quarter of the 20th century, and three species are believed to be extinct since 2000, including a species of macaw in Brazil and a Hawaiian crow. Conservation groups and governmental agencies have been raising an international alarm over the drop in bird populations, and partnerships have formed to counteract the trends. BirdLife went so far as to use the phrase "devastating extinction wave" in a recent statement. "If we continue to degrade and destroy vast areas of natural habitats then it will be difficult to prevent a much larger and more devastating extinction wave from washing over the continents."

As the lone survivors of the extinction event that killed off the dinosaurs 66 million years ago, birds have shown themselves to be among the most adaptive and resilient species on the planet. But just as science comes closer to understanding the full breadth of avian abilities, and how neurologically similar they are to humans, the relentless expansion of civilization has eliminated three billion birds from North America alone in the last 50 years. There's little doubt that seed-bearing migratory birds inspired the original concept of farming, yet today the agricultural industry continues to wreak havoc on bird populations, largely by killing off their insect prey. Our distant ancestors would stand in horrified judgment at humanity's utter disrespect for birds, the very creatures who taught us to speak and sing, who led us around the world to discover one Garden of Eden after another, and who were entrusted with the care of our immortal souls. Environmental activists say it's not too late to reverse the trends, but the clock is ticking.

Hope is the thing with feathers –
That perches in the soul –
And sings the tune without the words –
And never stops – at all …
– Emily Dickinson

Afterword

A Final Mystery

I never set out to write this book. There was no plan to compose an epic narrative, no preparation for a deep dive into the ecological roots of myth and religion.

While conducting research for a slim novel of historical fiction, I toured the megalithic mounds in Ireland's Boyne Valley in May 2014 and photographed dozens of massive kerbstones covered with Neolithic art. The tour guide related an ancient Irish legend about people shapeshifting into swans and singing beautiful music, further noting that a flock of whooper swans still winters in the Boyne Valley, though much diminished from the days when the legend was first told. My focus was on the mound known as Brú na Bóinne, built about 5,200 years ago with a 60-foot passage leading to a central chamber that's still illuminated by the dawning sun on the winter solstice. While researching other structures aligned to the winter solstice sunrise, and aware of the close relationship between Gaelic and Sanskrit, I came across the Sun Temple at *Konârak* on the northeast coast of India, and soon found it was located next to the massive Lake Chilika, the largest wintering ground for migratory birds on the entire subcontinent.

Soon I had a growing list of temples aligned to the winter solstice that were built on the wintering grounds of migratory birds. The immediate problem was it was too much nonfiction to cram into *People of the Flow*, the intergenerational family saga I was trying to finish, so the list would have to wait. When the novel was done and out the door, my journalist personality took over and I picked up the list again along with what turned out to be the biggest ball of yarn I'd ever come across. It just kept unraveling, like a story that wanted to be told.

Somewhere along the way I looked through the pictures I'd

taken in the Boyne Valley and lingered on a kerbstone from Knowth that had far more complex features than any other. At center was what appeared to be a semi-circular sun, like rays dawning on the horizon, which I knew to be the symbol on the flag of the Fianna, the law enforcement arm of ancient Ireland. But Knowth was even older than Brú na Bóinne and both were built about 2,000 years before the Celts arrived, so the parallel must be coincidental.

A closer look revealed several curious features. Above a straight horizontal line near the top, the stone was much darker. The top of the stone was flat, but the bottom had clearly been shaped into a triangle, with the tip buried in the ground and out of view. Taken together, these features suggested the stone had been turned upside down from its original position. The stain across the flat 'top' of the stone suggested it may have been partially buried in the ground or submerged in a pool. The V-shaped 'bottom' of the stone, now buried in the ground, could have been used as a sightline like the triangular stone at Beltany Tops, as reported by archaeologist Aubrey Burl. I knew the builders of Knowth and the two other mounds had abandoned the sites within a thousand years or so, and I soon learned that when Neolithic peoples abandoned sacred sites, they practiced an unknown series of rituals to "shut off" the connection to the cosmos. Maybe the kerbstone had been turned upside down to hide its secrets.

Inspired to further research, I found this particular kerbstone was known as K-17 and was the subject of a book that claimed it was the oldest sundial ever found, as reported on the website Knowth.com. As far as I could tell the author was an independent researcher who at some point had left Europe and couldn't be contacted. There was no mention of the kerbstone being upside-down, which would be an important factor for a sundial. I discussed the matter with my friend Geoff Ward, whom I'd met at a reunion concert of Dr. Strange and the Strangelies in Castletownbere, County Cork. Geoff was a journalist in Britain for much of his adult life and is now an author and writer for

Medium and other outlets, who also plays guitar and sings in the local establishments of Castletownbere, sometimes with his wife Angie, who plays the pipe. Geoff has long been fascinated by the megaliths of Europe and ancient cultures in general and is part of an online community of like-minded people.

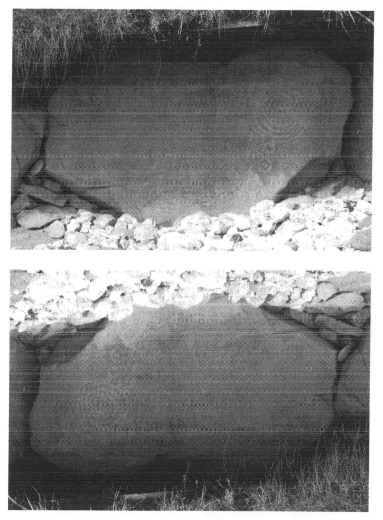

Above is K-17 as it appears at Knowth. Below the photo is flipped upside down. Photo by Ben Gagnon.

I told Geoff that when I flipped the photograph of K-17 upside-down on my computer, it seemed clear that the stone had been turned upside down at some point in time. No other kerbstone had a flat stain like K-17, and to my eye the smoothness of the stain suggested water. Maybe the bottom of the stone was submerged at one end of a shallow pool. Looking at the photographs, Geoff agreed the stain was unusual. If the image on the stone was meant to be reflected in a shallow pool, then the whole set-up could have been a ritualistic method of scrying, in which druids stared into still water to see the future. In this case they would be staring at the reflected image of the rays of a rising sun. But there was more to it.

Right in the middle of the radiating lines on K-17 are two inset cupules that sparked a memory. The nearby Hall of Tara was once described as opulently decorated with hammered gold and gems that no one would dare touch, much less try to steal. Perhaps gems were embedded in the cupules of K-17 and were intended to refract the dawn sunlight into colors that flashed over the shallow pool. Submerging a few heated stones in the pool would cause steam to rise and catch the colors of the rainbow, creating the perfect druidic atmosphere for predicting the future. About 4,000 years ago, the druids of the British Isles and Ireland practiced divination by staring into polished beryl, quartz, black glass, and still water, according to accounts from Julius Caesar and the Roman writer Pliny the Elder. The practice of scrying was depicted on 6,000-year-old murals in ancient Egypt and was practiced by the kings of ancient Persia by staring into the Cup of Jamshid. Admittedly, this elaborate scenario involving K-17 is built on rather threadbare circumstantial evidence. Geoff agreed it was a narrow bridge of clues, but interesting enough to pursue.

Another intriguing aspect of K-17 was the faint outline of what appeared to be a swan to the right of the radiating sun. I figured the image had gone unnoticed because the stone been upside down for a very long time. My thought process was simple: It might not be a swan at all, but it could be. To the right of the radiating sun, the swan appears to be shown in profile with its head facing left. The eye is over-large, but the lines of the head seem clear, while lower down are lines that suggest a curving neck. It could certainly be a case of pareidolia, in which my brain constructed a pattern I expected or hoped to see in a random maze of cracks. And there's nothing else like it in the area. If it's really a swan on K-17, it would be the only naturalistic image in the Boyne Valley, where the Neolithic art is made up of spirals, concentric circles, diamond-shapes, wavy lines, cross-hatching, and other geometric forms.

On the other hand, a swan carved in stone on the wintering grounds of swans would not be surprising in itself. Maybe K-17 wasn't decorated by the dark-skinned farmers who arrived in the Boinne Valley from the Near East about 6,000 years ago, according to genetic studies, and likely built the three megalithic mounds. Perhaps the stone was carved much later by the Celts, who arrived long after the area was abandoned by the original builders. Maybe K-17 was used by the Celts in a stand-alone fashion as speculated above and then after the last pagan king surrendered at Tara 1,500 years ago, it was turned upside down and hidden among the kerbstones of Knowth. Or perhaps it was a case of pareidolia coupled with delusions of grandeur. After all, discovering the first evidence of Celts in the megalithic remains of the Boyne Valley would be big news. That's a lot of maybes.

The strongest evidence is the stain and the shape of the stone, both suggesting that at some point K-17 was turned upside down. I'm happy to leave the possibility of a swan image to the experts. So Geoff and I wrote a letter to the powers that be in charge of the Boyne Valley site, laying out our case and asking that K-17 undergo forensic archaeological tests to determine what the stain was all about. At the same time, Geoff wrote an article on the subject for *Medium* in July 2019, which attracted 2,300 "views" and 835 "reads," along with hundreds of comments on Facebook.

While our letter requesting forensic tests went unanswered, the article attracted a response from Anthony Murphy, a photographer and researcher specializing in the Boyne Valley. He wrote that there was no swan image on K-17, and that whatever people might be seeing was only random cracks in the stone. He also produced an infrared photo of the stone that showed no trace of the swan image. Perhaps an infrared photo in this case is definitive in some way, but I can't help thinking that the people who decorated K-17 never saw it in the infrared spectrum. Whatever they were trying to communicate was in the regular visual spectrum. Overall, what bothered me about Murphy's response was he didn't address the stain on the stone, the shape of the top and bottom of the stone, and the question of whether it had been intentionally turned upside down.

Meanwhile this daisy chain of a story has one more chapter to unfold, and it's perhaps the most tenuous chain of all, more like a swaying rope bridge, but it does bring a boatload of circumstantial context to the swan image on K-17.

If one or more druids stood behind K-17 and gazed over the stone at its reflection in a pool, the image of the swan's head would appear at the upper left, facing the semicircular, halfway risen sun. It was a motif I'd seen somewhere before. There was a meaning behind the arch with a bird at the upper left, at about 10 o'clock relative to the arch. It was the same position as Cygnus relative to the U-shaped neck of Draco in the northern sky during the winter solstice. It was a cosmic clock that even a child could track by looking at the night sky. Like any other important day on the sacred calendar, it would make sense for the winter solstice to have its own symbol that everyone could recognize. Each day as the solstice approached, the cosmic alignment everyone was waiting for fell steadily into place, like a countdown before the big day. Some of the most compelling examples of the motif include:

- A Celtic image of the sun god Apollo on the 2,100-year-old Gundestrup Cauldron, discovered in Denmark. The god's head is inside an arch-shaped headdress, and he's touching a bird at 10 o'clock with his right hand. The headdress may be a symbol of hair, which was commonly equated with flowing water in ancient cultures.
- A 4,300-year-old Akkadian cylinder seal shows a Sumerian creator god inside the bend of an arch-shaped river, touching a bird at 10 o'clock with his right hand. Left of center and below a winged, one-footed goddess is a man holding a jagged knife, a symbol identified by scholars as the sun rising over the jagged Zagros Mountains to the east.
- Ancient Egyptian murals of the goddess Net show her as the embodiment of the Milky Way with her body bent in a U-shaped arch. In at least two murals, a bird is depicted at 10 o'clock relative to the bending goddess, who was said to mythically give birth to the sun.
- A wooden carving of Jesus dating to the early Christian church in Armenia features an arch shape around the deity's head, in this case representing the radiance of Christ. The motif is completed by a dove at 10'clock, also with a halo, indicating the Holy Spirit.
- The Fremont culture occupied much of Utah between 1,400 and 700 years ago and is primarily known for its rock art, including a pictograph showing a large arch (in a similar style as the Gundestrup Cauldron) with an owl at 10 o'clock. The Fremont buried stuffed owls with their dead, and caught owls, raptors, and ravens to use their feathers as personal decorations and sacred ornaments.
- In Aztec culture the winter solstice was the birthday of the sun god Huitzilopochtli, a day when human sacrifices

well exceeded the norm. The Codex Megliabecchi includes a painting of a human sacrifice dedicated to Huitzilopochtli in which the victim is bent backwards to form an arch shape, with an unmistakable bird symbol at 10 o'clock. Behind the priest is an archway leading to the inner sanctum of the temple.

There are numerous other examples of the arch-bird motif, echoing the much older bird-serpent symbolism that's found across cultures. Does this context mean the image on K-17 is a swan at the upper left of an arch formed by a semi-circular rising sun? Technically no. The image could still be a maze of cracks. Or it could be the oldest example of a cross-cultural winter solstice motif that's been around for more than 5,000 years, possibly created by immigrants from the Near East, or by Celts from the Eurasian Steppe who later followed the River Danube to western Europe. Other examples of the same motif can be found in the ancient Near East (the Akkadian seal) and in Celtic culture (the Gundestrup Cauldron).

It may be obvious by now why this tale of a possible swan glyph at Knowth was not included in the body of this book. No matter how compelling it is to me and others fascinated by the Neolithic and Celtic cultures of Europe, the evidence was just too sketchy to make the final cut. But I still remember the afternoon when I flipped my photo of K-17 upside down and saw what looked like a swan, and I still hope someone in authority will initiate a study of the mysterious stain.

World Trees: Ecological Traits and Religious Symbolism

The following are 14 additional examples of world trees chosen by cultures around the globe to represent the axis of the world, connecting Earth to the spirit world in the cosmos. A full review of the biological traits often found in world trees and the religious symbolism they reflect can be found in Chapter 7, along with an initial 12 examples.

Apple

Biology/Ecology: The apple tree has oval leaves and can grow up to 30 feet in the wild, producing 5-petaled white flowers in spring and mature apples in autumn. Originating in Central Asia and northwestern China, the apple tree has spread around the world.

Religious/Medicinal: The apple tree appears in Irish myths describing the timeless heaven of Tir na Nog, where its silver branches and purple crystal blooms are accompanied by constant birdsong. Shaking the branch of a magical apple tree produced music to soothe the soul. Like remote groves of yew, apple groves were a destination for men to find comfort and healing after being psychically damaged in battle. The legendary Irish King Connla visited the mythic island where the original divine apple tree grew, and during his trip was continually sustained by a single apple that reappeared every time he ate it. On another legendary voyage, Maol Duin brought along the rod of an apple tree that produced enough apples to feed the whole crew. The Norse goddess Freya was associated with the apple tree.

White Poplar

Biology/Ecology: Native to the rivers of Morocco, Spain, central Europe and Central Asia, the white poplar grows up to 100 feet and is resistant to floodwaters. Its bark is white with grey and green tints, the young shoots and buds are covered in white down, and the young leaves are covered in a white crust. At maturity the leaves are green on top and white underneath. Birds love to feed on the white poplar's cottony seeds.

Religious/Medicinal: In Greco-Roman mythology, the poplar was the daughter of Oceanus, the mythic river that encircled the world. Although the poplar goddess was abducted to the underworld, the gods in turn caused a poplar to grow in the Elysian Fields of the upper (spirit) world. The Greeks celebrated the poplar's green and white leaves as a symbol of universal duality, and were carved on the base of a statue in a sanctuary to Herakles along the Tiber River.

European Mountain Ash

Biology/Ecology: The European Mountain Ash has smooth grey bark and blooms white flowers in late spring. It will regenerate branches after coppicing. Its red fruit ripens in late summer and is eaten by birds before their winter migration.

Religious/Medicinal: In Norse mythology, a giant ash known as Yggdrasil was the world tree. A mythic bird was said to live in its branches while a serpent guarded the base. Odin gained wisdom by hanging upside down in its branches. Concoctions using the tree's ovate leaves were used to cure snake bites, leprosy, jaundice, kidney stones, warts, ringworm, and earache.

Common Fig

Biology/Ecology: First cultivated along the Sea of Galilee about 23,000 years ago, the common fig runs with white sap and is found from the Mediterranean to West Asia. Inside the fruit are white flowers, where wasps crawl and emerge covered with white pollen.

Religious/Medicinal: The Babylonian goddess Ishtar took the form of a fig tree known as Xikum, the "primeval mother at the central place of the earth." In Greek myth, Odysseus held on to the branch of a fig to avoid being sucked into a whirlpool created by a sea monster. The common fig was widely used as a medicinal plant, and was recently found to be effective against bacteria, parasites, and tumors.

Umbrella Thorn Acacia

Biology/Ecology: Native to Africa and growing up to 70 feet tall, the umbrella thorn acacia is able to grow in virtually any environment, tolerating drought, frost, high temperatures, and acidic and sandy soils. Although its lifespan is only 30 years, the acacia's toughness makes it a species that grows in damaged landscapes. A common tree of the African savanna, the acacia produces tight bunches of white and very fragrant flowers in summer.

Religious/Medicinal: Perhaps the acacia's apparent invulnerability was the reason it was used exclusively to build the Hebrew Tabernacle (portable Tent of the Congregation) and the Ark of the Covenant. Acacia roots, shoots, and gum have been used as tools, decorations, and medicine. It's taboo to cut down the acacia in South Africa.

Somb

Biology/Ecology: Native to West Africa and reaching 65 feet in height, the bark of the somb is reddish-brown with white streaks. Its fragrant spring flowers are greenish-white to yellow.

Religious/Medicinal: The creation myth of the Serer people of Senegal begins with the supreme being creating the somb tree in the primordial swamp of earth. Thought to be the ancestor of all plant life, the somb tree's hard, rot-resistant wood was used to build burial chambers, which have remained intact for more than a thousand years. In traditional medicine, the leaves are used for headaches, the bark is an astringent used to treat skin diseases and fevers, and the roots are used to treat gonorrhea, dysentery and bronchitis.

Ashoka

Biology/Ecology: Native to India, the evergreen ashoka tree blooms in very fragrant red, orange, yellow, or white flowers from February to April.

Religious/Medicinal: The yakshini is an ancient and voluptuous female tree spirit often appearing on either side of a gateway to Hindu and Buddhist temples. In an alluring pose with her foot on the trunk, the yakshini grasps a branch of the ashoka, infusing it with a generative quality that causes it to bloom. Legend has it that Queen Māyā gave birth to Gautama Buddha under an ashoka tree, while grasping its branch. Every part of the tree cures a variety of ailments.

Neem

Biology/Ecology: Native to India and Southeast Asia and known as Neem the Healer to Hindus and Buddhists, the neem tree produces delicate white flowers in spring. Growing up to 65 feet, the neem tree's whitish-yellow fruit has a hard white shell around one or two seeds.

Religious/Medicinal: In Hindu mythology the neem tree has a cosmic origin: Its original seed was sprinkled to earth in the immortal elixir Amrita by divine beings. Every part of the tree has been used for medicinal purposes for more than 2,000 years.

White Mulberry

Biology/Ecology: Cultivation of the white mulberry tree as a habitat for white silkworms began more than 4,700 years ago in China, where the tree's white and yellow flowers bloom in spring. Its tiny fruits are purple in the wild but were bred to be white and pink. Likewise, silkworms make yellow silk in the wild but were bred to make white silk. Symbolic of rebirth, the silkworm weaves a cocoon around the ovate mulberry leaf, ultimately producing a white moth.

Religious/Medicinal: In Chinese mythology, the mulberry is the Fusang tree, a world tree that grows on a mysterious island in the Pacific Ocean where the sun rises. One of the 10 ravens living in Fusang's branches carried the sun to its apex each day.

(White) Paper Birch

Biology/Ecology: Native to North America, the paper birch grows up to 65 feet tall, with long, wide strips of bark easily removeable.

Religious/Medicinal: In the Ojibwe/Chippewa communities in the Great Lakes region, birchbark was a sacred gift from an ancestral hero used to cover canoes and shelters, and to ceremonially wrap the bodies of the dead. The birch tree is a clan symbol of the Pueblo tribes in New Mexico.

Flowering Dogwood

Biology/Ecology: A favorite of migratory birds, the flowering dogwood blooms in early spring with white petals around a yellow center, attracting insects for the newly arrived birds to feed on. In September and October, its red berries ripen and are fuel for birds getting ready for the fall migration. A good tree for nesting, the flowering dogwood attracts robins, bluebirds, thrushes, catbirds, cardinals, tanagers, and grosbeaks, among others.

Religious/Medicinal: For the Mohawk of northern New York and Canada, a giant dogwood was the primeval Tree of Life in the Sky World. Northwestern tribes such as the Quileute and Makah ate dogwood berries during religious ceremonies, and the dogwood's bark and roots were used in traditional medicine. There is a Dogwood clan in the Zuni tribe.

Cottonwood

Biology/Ecology: Growing up to 100 feet high, the cottonwood tree was sacred to Native Americans in the Southwest and Great Plains. The cottonwood has whitish cracked bark, heart-shaped leaves and its frizzy-white fruits easily blow in the wind.

Religious/Medicinal: The Hopi and Pueblo used cottonwood roots to make sacred dolls and masks, while tribes of the Great Plains used branches to make sacred poles. Others used the cottonwood to make drums and baskets, and as part of ritual cremations. In Navajo hogans, the trunk was one of the four sacred pillars that held up the home. The bark and leaves were used to treat wounds and swelling, while its inner bark (containing Vitamin C) was commonly chewed.

Eastern Red Cedar

Biology/Ecology: Known to live up to 900 years, the Eastern red cedar produces berries covered in white wax during winter that attract cedar waxwings, turkeys, mockingbirds, and warblers. From the Atlantic seaboard to the Southwest, the cedar's dense needles provide birds with shelter from weather and a good nesting location.

Religious/Medicinal: The trunk of the red cedar is one of the Navajo's four sacred pillars holding up the family Hogan. The Hopi identify the cedar as one of the chiefs of the world, while the Blackfoot of the Northern Plains used juniper branches in offerings to the sun. In Arizona, the Zuni prepared for the winter solstice by gathering cedar wood for bonfires.

White Spruce

Biology/Ecology: Native to North America and reaching 130 feet in height, the white spruce (with white bark) makes for a good shelter and nesting site for birds, specifically attracting finches in winter.

Religious/Medicinal: A Hopi legend tells of a medicine man who transformed into the first spruce tree, and one of their clans represents the spruce. In southern Arizona, the Pima creation story describes the father and mother of the Pima people surviving a flood by floating in a ball of spruce pitch. In the Pacific Northwest, the Makah's creation story includes the origin of the first spruce tree. Northern Algonquian tribes once bundled spruce and fir needles into herbal pillows to prevent illness.

Bibliography

Alexander, Hartley Burr, 2005, *Native American Mythology*, Dover Publications. (Originally 1916, *Mythology of all Races: North American*, Marshall Jones Company.)

Ashmore, Wendy, and Knapp, A. Bernard, eds, 1999, *Archaeologies of Landscape*, Blackwell Publishers.

Aveni, Anthony, 2019, *Star Stories: Constellations and People*, Yale University Press.

Baba, Ifa Karade, 1994, *The Handbook of Yoruba Religious Concepts*, Weiser Books.

Bailleul-LeSuer, Rozenn, ed., 2012, *Between Heaven and Earth: Birds in Ancient Egypt*, The Oriental Institute of the University of Chicago.

Barber, Elizabeth Wayland, and Barber, Paul T., 2005, *When They Severed Earth from Sky: How the Human Mind Shapes Myth*, Princeton University Press.

Baring, Anne, and Cashford, Jules, 1991, *The Myth of the Goddess: Evolution of an Image*, Viking Arkana.

Barker, Graeme; Goucher, Candice, 2015, *A World with Agriculture, 12,000 BCE—500 CE*, Cambridge University Press.

Barua, Benimadhab, 1998, *A History of Pre-Buddhistic Indian Philosophy*, Motilal Banarsidass Publishers (First edition, 1921).

Benson, J.L., 1996, *Horse, Bird & Man: The Origin of Greek Painting*, University of Massachusetts Press.

Bierlein, J.F., 1994, *Parallel Myths*, Ballantine Books.

Black Elk, Wallace, and Lyon, William S., 1990, *Black Elk: The Sacred Ways of a Lakota*, Harper & Row.

Boas, Franz, 1964, *The Central Eskimo*, University of Nebraska Press (orig. 1888 in report of Bureau of Ethnology, Smithsonian Institution).

Boehme, Madeleine, 2020, *Ancient Bones: Unearthing the*

Astonishing New Story of How We Became Human, Greystone Books.

Brazil, Mark, 2003, *The Whooper Swan*, T & A D Poyser.

Breverton, Terry, 2011, *Breverton's Phantasmagoria: A Compendium of Monsters, Myths and Legends*, Quercus Publishing.

Brown, Frank Burch (Ed.), 2014, *The Oxford Handbook of Religion and the Arts*, Oxford University Press.

Budge, E.A. Wallis, 1969, *The Gods of the Egyptians*, Dover Publications (orig. 1904).

Burger, L. Richard, 1992, *Chavin and the Origins of Andean Civilizations*, Thames & Hudson.

Burl, Aubrey, 1979, *Prehistoric Stone Circles*, Shire Publications.

Caldecott, Moyra, 1993, *Myths of the Sacred Tree*, Destiny Books.

Cavendish, Richard (Ed.), 1980, *Mythology: An Illustrated Encyclopedia*, Rizzoli International Publications.

Chittick, William C., 2005, *The Sufi Doctrine of Rumi*, World Wisdom.

Coitir, Niall Mac, 2003, *Irish Trees: Myths, Legends & Folklore*, The Collins Press.

Conze, Edward (Ed.), 1954, *Buddhist Texts Through the Ages*, Philosophical Library.

Cotterell, Arthur and Storm, Rachel, 2012, *The Ultimate Encyclopedia of Mythology*, Anness Publishing.

Craig, William Lane, 1980, *The Cosmological Argument: From Plato to Liebniz*, The Macmillan Press.

Curtis, Natalie, 1996, *The Indians Book*, Portland House (Orig. 1905).

Dames, Michael, 1992, *Mythic Ireland*, Thames and Hudson.

Dragomanov, M.P., 1961, *Notes on the Slavic Religio-Ethical Legends: The Dualistic Creation of the World*, Indiana University/ Mouton & Co.

Efuntade, Anthony Canty, 2013, *The Power of the Coconut and the Yoruba Religion*, Xlibris LLC.

Eliade, Mircea, 1957, *The Sacred and the Profane: The Nature of*

Religion, Harcourt Inc.

Eliade, Mircea, 1958, *Patterns in Comparative Religion*, Sheed & Ward, Inc.

Eliade, Mircea, 1964, *Shamanism: Archaic Techniques of Ecstasy*, Princeton University Press.

Emery, Nathan, 2016, *Bird Brain: An Exploration of Avian Intelligence*, Princeton University Press.

Erdoes, Richard and Ortiz, Alfonso, 1984, *American Indian Myths and Legends*, Pantheon Books.

Esposito, John L., 2003, *Great World Religions: Islam*, The Teaching Company.

Evans-Pritchard, E.E., 1965, *Theories of Primitive Religion*, Oxford University Press.

Evans Wentz, W.Y., 1911, *The Fairy-Faith in Celtic Countries*, Oxford University Press.

Felton, Todd R., 2007, *A Journey into Ireland's Literary Revival*, Roaring Forties Press.

Finlayson, Clive, 2019, *The Smart Neanderthal: Cave Art, Bird Catching, and the Cognitive Revolution*, Oxford University Press.

Firestone, Reuven, 1990, *Journeys in Holy Lands*, State University of New York Press.

Flood, Gavin and Martin, Charles (Translation), 2102, *The Bhagavad Gita*, W.W. Norton & Co.

Foster, Benjamin R., 1995 *From Distant Days: Myths, Tales and Poetry of Ancient Mesopotamia*, CDL Press.

Frazer, Sir James G., 2013, *The Great Flood: A Handbook of World Flood Myths*, JasonColavito.com Books (originally published by Macmillan and Co. in 1918 as Chapter Four in *Folklore of the Old Testament, Vol. 1*).

Frazer, Sir James, 1993, *The Golden Bough*, Wordsworth Editions.

Garnett, Jacqueline Ingalls, 2005, *Newgrange Speaks for Itself: Forty Carved Motifs*, Trafford Publishing.

Genceolu, Deniz, Ed., undated, *Actual Archaeology Magazine/*

Anatolia: *Understanding Gobekli Tepe*, (single-topic issue) Actual Archaeology Publishing, undated.

Gibson, Graeme, 2021, *The Bedside Book of Birds: An Avian Miscellany*, Doubleday.

Green, Alberto R. W., 2003, *The Storm God in the Ancient Near East*, Eisenbrauns.

Hackin, J. et al, 1963, *Asiatic Mythology*, Thomas Y. Crowell Company.

Hammond, Rose, *Islands in the Sky: The Four-Dimensional Journey of Odysseus through Space and Time*, 2013, Cambridge Scholars Publishing.

Hancock, Graham and Bauval, Robert, 1996, *The Message of the Sphinx: A Quest for the Hidden Legacy of Mankind*, Three River Publishing/Random House.

Hancock, Graham, 1998, *Heaven's Mirror: Quest for the Lost Civilization*, Three Rivers Press.

Hanh, Thich Nhat, 1992, *Old Path White Clouds*, Parallax Press.

Harner, Michael J., 1984, *The Jivaro: People of the Sacred Waterfalls*, University of California Press (first ed. 1972).

Harris, J. Rendel, 1925, *Apollo's Birds*, reprinted from *The Bulletin of the John Rylands Library*, Vol. 9, No. 2, July 1925.

Hobbs, Kevin, and West, David, 2020, *The Story of Trees and how they changed the way we live*, Laurence King Publishing.

Hopkins Hawkes, Jacquetta, 1974, *Atlas of Ancient Archaeology*, Michael O'Mara Books.

Hyde, Douglas, *A Literary History of Ireland: From Earliest Times to the Present Day*, 1903 (third impression), T. Fisher Unwin, Paternoster Square, London.

Ibrahim, Sliman Ben, 1918, *The Life of Mohammed: Prophet of Allah*, L'Edition D'Art.

Imbrogno, Philip J., 2019, *Strange Heavens*, Llewellyn Publications.

Ingersoll, Ernest, 1923, *Birds in Legend Fable and Folklore*, reprinted 2020; ed. Tarl Warwick.

Jamal, Mahmood (Ed.), 2009, *Islamic Mystical Poetry: Sufi Verse from the Early Mystics to Rumi*, Penguin Classics.

James, George Alfred, 1995, *Interpreting Religion: The Phenomenological Approaches of Pierre Daniel Chantepie de la Saussaye, W. Bede Kristensen and Gerardus van der Leeuw*, The Catholic University of America Press.

James, William, 2012, *The Varieties of Religious Experience: A Study of Human Nature*, ReadAClassic.com (originally 1902).

Jones, David M., and Molyneaux, Brian L., 2011, *Mythology of the American Nations*, Anness Publishing.

Joyce, P.W., 1879, *Old Celtic Romances: Tales from Irish Mythology*, David Nutt (London).

Karuna Sagar Behera, *Konark: The Black Pagoda*, 2005, Publications Division, Government of India (originally Saka 1926).

Kearns, Hugh, *Newgrange: The Mystery of the Chequered Lights*, 1993, Elo Publications.

Keating, Geoffrey, 2012 (reprint), *Keating's History of Ireland*, General Books.

Khan, Pir Vilayat Inayat, 1999, *Awakening: A Sufi Experience*, Penguin Putnam.

Knoblock, John and Riegel, Jeffrey (translators), 2000 *The Annals of Lu Buwei*, Stanford University Press.

Kroeber, A.L. *The Handbook of the Indians of California*, 1976, Dover Publications (*Bulletin 78*, 1925, Bureau of American Ethnology, Smithsonian Institution).

Kristensen, Brede, W. 1960, *The Meaning of Religion*, Martinus Nijhoff / The Hague.

Lake-Thom, Bobby, 1997, *Spirits of the Earth: A Guide to Native American Nature Symbols, Stories and Ceremonies*, Penguin Group.

Lang, Andrew, *The Making of Religion*, 1898, Longmans, Green, and Co.

Lang, Andrew, 2008, *Myth, Ritual and Religion: Volume I*, Dodo Press (first edition, 1887).

Lang, Andrew, 1901, *Myth, Ritual and Religion, Volume 2*,

Longmans, Green, and Co. (orig. 1887).

Leach, Maria, 1956, *The Beginning: Creation Myths Around the World*, Funk & Wagnalls.

Leeming, David and Margaret, 1994, *A Dictionary of Creation Myths*, Oxford University Press.

Lewis-Williams, David and Pearce, David, 2005, *Inside the Neolithic Mind*, Thames & Hudson.

Lockyer, Norman, *The Dawn of Astronomy: A Study of Temple Worship and Mythology of the Ancient Egyptians*, 1894, Cassell and Company.

Long, Charles H., 1963, *Alpha: The Myths of Creation*, George Braziller, Inc.

Mac Coitir, Niall, 2003, *Irish Trees: Myths, Legends & Folklore*, The Collins Press.

Mackenzie, Donald A., 1926, *Migration of Symbols*, Alfred A. Knopf.

Macpherson, James // Burnett, Allan & Burnett, Linda A., (Ed.), 2011, *Blind Ossian's Fingal: Fragments and Controversies*, Luath Press Limited (originally *Fragments of Ancient Poetry*, 1760).

Magli, Giulio, 2020, *Archaeoastronomy: Introduction to the Science of Stars and Stones*, Springer.

Major, John S.; Queen, Sarah A.; Meyer, Andrew Seth; Roth, Harold D., 2012, *The Essential Huainanzi*, Columbia University Press.

Malville, J. McKim, 2008, *Guide to Prehistoric Astronomy in the Southwest*, Johnson Books, imprint of Bower House, Denver.

Maryboy, Nancy C., Begay, David, *Sharing the Skies: Navajo Astronomy*, Rio Nuevo Publishers.

Mathews, John, 1991, *Taliesin: The Last Celtic Shaman*, Inner Traditions.

Mayor, Adrienne, 2005, *Fossil Legends of the First Americans*, Princeton University Press.

McIntosh, Christopher, 2019, *Beyond the North Wind: The Fall and Rise of the Mystic North*, Weiser Books.

Melora Correal, Tobe, 2003, *Finding Soul on the Path of Orisa*, Crossing Press, Berkeley.

Miller, Dorcas S., 1997, *Stars of the First People: Native American Star Myths and Constellations*, Pruett Publishing Company.

Miller, Moshe, 2000, *Zohar*, Fiftieth Gate Publications and Seminars.

Moure, Ramon Dacal, and De La Calle, Manuel Rivero, 1996, *Art and Archaeology of Pre-Columbian Cuba*, University of Pittsburgh Press.

Murphy, Anthony, 2012, *Newgrange: Monument to Immortality*, The Liffey Press.

Mynott, Jeremy, 2018, *Birds in the Ancient World*, Oxford University Press.

Nadeau, Randall, Essay on *Yin-Yang Souls and Spirits*, Trinity University website.

Narayan, R. K., 1978, *The Mahabharata,* The University of Chicago Press.

Nathan, Leonard (translated by), 1976, *The Transport of Love: The Meghaduta of Kalidasa*, University of California Press.

Naydler, Jeremy, 2005, *Shamanic Wisdom in the Pyramid Texts: The Mystical Tradition of Ancient Egypt*, Inner Traditions.

Newton, Ian, 2013, *Bird Populations*, HarperCollins Publishers.

North, Carolyn, 2009, *In the Beginning: Creation Myths from around the World*, ICRL Press.

O'Grady, Standish, 1881, *History of Ireland; Critical and Philosophical Vol. 1*, Sampson Low & Co.

O'Kelly, Claire, 1967, *Illustrated Guide to Newgrange*, C. O'Kelly.

O'Kelly, Michael J., 1982, *Newgrange: Archeology, Art and Legend*, Thames and Hudson.

Otto, Rudolph, 1917, *The Idea of the Holy*, Oxford University Press.

Panda, Dr. Narasingha Charan, 2010, *The Life of Gautama Buddha*, Bharatiya Kala Prakashan.

Pennick, Nigel, 1997, *The Celtic Saints*, Sterling Publishing Co.

Plate, S. Brent, 2014, *A History of Religion in 5 1/2 Objects*, Beacon Press.

Presley, Gail M., 2000, *The Philosophical Quest: A Cross-Cultural Reader*, McGraw-Hill Higher Education, including Herbert John Benally, *Navajo Ways of Knowing*; Sarvepalli Radhakrishnan, *The Religious Experience*; and Gregory Baum, *Social Conceptions of Death*.

Preus, J. Samuel, 1996, *Explaining Religion: Criticism and Theory from Bodin to Freud*, Scholars Press.

Reina, Ruben E., and Kensinger, Kenneth M., eds., 1991, *The Gift of Birds: Featherwork of Native South American People*, Museum of Archaeology and Anthropology, University of Pennsylvania.

Rhie and Thurman, 1999, *Worlds of Transformation: Tibetan Art of Wisdom and Compassion*, Tibet House.

Radhakrishnan, Sarvepalli, and Moore, Charles A., 1957, *A Sourcebook in Indian Philosophy*, Princeton University Press.

Rappenglück, Michael A., "Heavenly Messengers: The Role of Birds in the Cosmographies and Cosmovisions of Ancient Cultures," a paper given during the 2009 conference, "Cosmologies Across Cultures" at Gilching Observatory in Germany.

Rolleston, T.W., 1911, *Myths and Legends of the Celtic Race*, Thomas Y. Crowell Company.

Rowland, Beryl, 1978, *Birds with Human Souls, A Guide to Bird Symbolism*, University of Tennessee Press/Knoxville.

de Santillana, Giorgia, and von Dechend, Hertha, 1969, *Hamlet's Mill: An Essay on Myth and the Frame of Time*, Gambit.

Schmidt, Wilhelm, *The Origin and Growth of Religion*, 2014, Wythe-North Publishing (orig. Eng. edition 1931; German edition, 1912).

Shah, Idries, 1968, *The Way of the Sufi*, London: Jonathan Cape.

Sheehy, Jeanne, 1980, *The Rediscovery of Ireland's Past: The Celtic Revival 1830 -1930*, Thames and Hudson.

Siskin, Edgar E., 1983, *Washo Shamans and Peyotists*, University of Utah Press.

Sjoestedt, Marie-Louise, 2000, *Celtic Gods and Heroes*, Dover Publications (first edition 1949, Methuen & Co. Ltd.).

Smith, Huston, 1958, *The World's Religions*, HarperCollins.

Solecki, Ralph S. et al, 2004, *The Proto-Neolithic Cemetery at Shanidar Cave*, Texas A&M University Press.

Spencer, Herbert, 1896, *The Principles of Sociology: Volume I*, University Press of the Pacific (2004 reprint).

Sproul, Barbara C., 1991, *Primal Myths*, HarperCollins.

Strom, Robert, Ed., *Guardians of the Sun-Door: Late Iconographic Essays & Drawings of Ananda K. Coomaraswamy*, 2004, Vons Fitae.

Swami Prabhupada, A. C. Bhaktivedanta, *Bhagavad-Gita As Is*, 1983.

Sykes, Rebecca Wragg, 2020, *Kindred: Neanderthal Life, Love, Death and Art*, Bloomsbury Sigma.

Taves, Ann, 1999, *Fits, Trances & Visions: Experiencing Religion and Explaining Experience from Wesley to James*, Princeton University Press.

Tulku, Sharpa, Guard, Richard and Berzin, Alexander, 1990, *Victory Over Evil: Meditation on Vajrabahairava*, Library of Tibetan Works and Archives.

Turner, Patricia, and Coulter, Charles Russell, 2000, *Dictionary of Ancient Deities*, McFarland & Company Inc., Publishers.

Tylor, Sir Edward Burnett, 1958, *The Origins of Culture*, Harper Torchbooks (orig. *Primitive Culture Volume I*, 1871).

Tylor, Edward Burnett, 2012, *Primitive Culture*, Forgotten Books (orig. *Primitive Culture Volume II*, 1871).

Van Der Leeuw, Gerardus, 1963, *Sacred and Profane Beauty: The Holy in Art*, Abingdon Press.

Verpoorte, Alexander, 2001, *Places of Art, Traces of Fire: A contextual approach to anthropomorphic figurines in the Pavlovian (Central Europe, 29-24 kyr BP)*, Leiden University.

Von Franz, Marie-Louise, 1995, *Creation Myths, Revised Edition*,

Shambhala.

Waley, Arthur, 1958, *The Way and its Power: A Study of the Tao Te Ching and its Place in Chinese Thought*, Grove Press.

Walker, Gabrielle, 2007, *An Ocean of Air: Why the Wind Blows and other Mysteries of the Atmosphere*, Harcourt Inc.

Wallis, Glenn (transl), 2007, *The Dhammapada: Verses on the Way*, Modern Library.

Wang, Robin R., 2012, *Yinyang: The Way of Heaven and Earth in Chinese Thought and Culture*, Cambridge University Press.

Watts, Alan, *Erotic Spirituality: The Vision of Konârak* 1971, Collier Press.

Watts, Alan, 1975, *Tao: The Watercourse Way*, Pantheon Books.

Werner, E.T.C., 2010, *Myths and Legends of China*, Digireads.com Publishing.

Wilkins, W.J., 1900, *Hindu Mythology, Vedic and Puranic*, W. Thacker & Co.

Williams, Mike, 2010, *Prehistoric Belief: Shamans, Trances and the Afterlife*, The History Press

Wintemberg, W.J., *Myths and Fancies of the Milky Way*, Journal of the Royal Astronomical Society of Canada, Vol. 2, p.235.

Witzel, E.J. Michael, 2012, *The Origins of the World's Mythologies*, Oxford University Press.

Wong, Eva, 2001, *Tales of the Taoist Immortals*, Shambhala.

Wong, Eva, 2011, *Taoism: An Essential Guide*, Shambhala Publications.

Znamenski, Andrei A., 2007, *The Beauty of the Primitive: Shamanism and the Western Imagination*, Oxford University Press.

MOON
BOOKS
PAGANISM & SHAMANISM

What is Paganism? A religion, a spirituality, an alternative belief system, nature worship? You can find support for all these definitions (and many more) in dictionaries, encyclopaedias, and text books of religion, but subscribe to any one and the truth will evade you. Above all Paganism is a creative pursuit, an encounter with reality, an exploration of meaning and an expression of the soul. Druids, Heathens, Wiccans and others, all contribute their insights and literary riches to the Pagan tradition. Moon Books invites you to begin or to deepen your own encounter, right here, right now.
If you have enjoyed this book, why not tell other readers by posting a review on your preferred book site.

Recent bestsellers from Moon Books are:

Journey to the Dark Goddess
How to Return to Your Soul
Jane Meredith
Discover the powerful secrets of the Dark Goddess and
transform your depression, grief and pain into healing
and integration.
Paperback: 978-1-84694-677-6 ebook: 978-1-78099-223-5

Shamanic Reiki
Expanded Ways of Working with Universal Life Force Energy
Llyn Roberts, Robert Levy
Shamanism and Reiki are each powerful ways of healing; together,
their power multiplies. *Shamanic Reiki* introduces techniques to
help healers and Reiki practitioners tap ancient healing wisdom.
Paperback: 978-1-84694-037-8 ebook: 978-1-84694-650-9

Pagan Portals – The Awen Alone
Walking the Path of the Solitary Druid
Joanna van der Hoeven
An introductory guide for the solitary Druid, *The Awen Alone* will
accompany you as you explore, and seek out your own place
within the natural world.
Paperback: 978-1-78279-547-6 ebook: 978-1-78279-546-9

A Kitchen Witch's World of Magical Herbs & Plants
Rachel Patterson
A journey into the magical world of herbs and plants, filled with
magical uses, folklore, history and practical magic. By popular
writer, blogger and kitchen witch, Tansy Firedragon.
Paperback: 978-1-78279-621-3 ebook: 978-1-78279-620-6

Medicine for the Soul
The Complete Book of Shamanic Healing
Ross Heaven
All you will ever need to know about shamanic healing and how to become your own shaman...
Paperback: 978-1-78099-419-2 ebook: 978-1-78099-420-8

Shaman Pathways – The Druid Shaman
Exploring the Celtic Otherworld
Danu Forest
A practical guide to Celtic shamanism with exercises and techniques as well as traditional lore for exploring the Celtic Otherworld.
Paperback: 978-1-78099-615-8 ebook: 978-1-78099-616-5

Traditional Witchcraft for the Woods and Forests
A Witch's Guide to the Woodland with Guided Meditations and Pathworking
Mélusine Draco
A Witch's guide to walking alone in the woods, with guided meditations and pathworking.
Paperback: 978-1-84694-803-9 ebook: 978-1-84694-804-6

Wild Earth, Wild Soul
A Manual for an Ecstatic Culture
Bill Pfeiffer
Imagine a nature-based culture so alive and so connected, spreading like wildfire. This book is the first flame...
Paperback: 978-1-78099-187-0 ebook: 978-1-78099-188-7

Naming the Goddess
Trevor Greenfield
Naming the Goddess is written by over eighty adherents and
scholars of Goddess and Goddess Spirituality.
Paperback: 978-1-78279-476-9 ebook: 978-1-78279-475-2

Shapeshifting into Higher Consciousness
Heal and Transform Yourself and Our World with Ancient
Shamanic and Modern Methods
Llyn Roberts
Ancient and modern methods that you can use every day to
transform yourself and make a positive difference in the world.
Paperback: 978-1-84694-843-5 ebook: 978-1-84694-844-2

Readers of ebooks can buy or view any of these bestsellers by
clicking on the live link in the title. Most titles are published in
paperback and as an ebook. Paperbacks are available in traditional
bookshops. Both print and ebook formats are available online.

Find more titles and sign up to our readers' newsletter at
http://www.johnhuntpublishing.com/paganism
Follow us on Facebook at https://www.facebook.com/MoonBooks
and Twitter at https://twitter.com/MoonBooksJHP